"Liturgists and catechists, take note of this small book. It's a practical resource for enhancing the Sunday and holy day celebrations."

The Catholic Standard

"Bernadette Snyder and Hazelmai Terry believe that every Sunday is a special occasion. Their book suggests appropriate decor for every week of the year."

Jim Breig
Bringing Religion Home

"Here is a book that can be instrumental in helping parishes and schools enhance worship experiences tastefully and simply....special liturgies and special decorations can give the parish and students something to look forward to and remember....The many ideas in this book may serve as inspirations to help you see the possibilities of using everyday things just as Jesus did with his parables—to speak the language of God's love more clearly....Teachers may adapt the decorating ideas to use in the classrooms to highlight special occasions. Homemakers will discover ways to use these suggestions as table decorations for family meals celebrating special days."

Sr. Alice Doll, OSF
St. Cloud Visitor

"...offers a wealth of excellent ideas....I found the lenten section quite fascinating. Many of the others will supply a great deal of information to parish liturgy groups seeking seasonal decorations and themes to use....a fine book."

Sr. Victoria
Victory Noll

CYCLE A

DECORATING
For Sundays & Holy Days

Bernadette McCarver Snyder & Hazelmai McCarver Terry

XXIII
TWENTY-THIRD PUBLICATIONS
Mystic, Connecticut

Twenty-Third Publications
185 Willow Street
P.O. Box 180
Mystic, CT 06355
(203) 536-2611

ISBN 0-89622-416-3
Library of Congress Catalog Card No. 89-85346

DEDICATION

We dedicate this book to William Ransom Terry
(whom we still affectionately call Billy)—
a very special son and nephew
who we've watched grow from an
ever-smiling muddy-faced tot
playing with his muddy-pawed dog
or stirring up a bucketful of dreams in a sand pile
to a handsome and wise husband and father.

With Love from Mama and Aunt Bernadette

CONTENTS

INTRODUCTION

Why offer a "decorating" book that suggests themes, homily suggestions, parish activities, and altar decorations based on the Scripture readings for the Sundays and holy days in Cycle A? Does the Mass really need embellishments and extras? Of course not. In essence, the Mass is complete and perfect in itself, but perhaps some of the people in the pews need "adornments"—to help draw their attention away from the outside world, to focus on the moment and the celebration and invite them to a deeper prayer of community.

The document, *Environment and Art in Catholic Worship,* issued by the Bishops' Committee on the Liturgy, explains that although God cannot "be contained in or confined by words or images," liturgical symbols can be "avenues of approach."

The bishops' document further states:

> God does not need liturgy; people do, and people have only their own arts and styles of expression with which to celebrate. Like the covenant itself, the liturgical celebrations of the faith community (church) involve the whole person. They are not purely religious or merely rational and intellectual exercises, but also human experiences calling on all human faculties: body, mind, senses, imagination, emotions, memory.

The effectiveness of this "whole person" approach first became evident to me when I was teaching first-grade religion classes. The children were fresh and innocent and excited about God—but they were of the television generation, accustomed to visual as well as oral instruction. I soon discovered that any kind of visual aid increased the likelihood that they would remember and profit from the day's lesson. For example, when I talked about the Last Supper, I set a table with a tablecloth, flowers, etc. and we sat around it and shared matzoh crackers and grape juice as we talked about Jesus and his apostles, the bread and wine, the body and blood. Later, when I quizzed them about the eucharist, they remembered not only the meal but its meaning.

Today many busy people have only one "religious encounter" during the week, when they come to Mass on Saturday evening or on Sunday. The Scripture readings of the Mass should give them a message to last through the remainder of the week, a nugget of hope and inspiration to live by, but do they remember those important readings? Even if you asked them immediately after Mass—at the door of church or in the parking lot—many would be unable to recall any of the Scripture passages of the day.

These suggestions for altar decorations and parish activities are just a visual way to re-emphasize the readings so that it will be easier for the people to remember them and perhaps act on them during the week. The "embellishments" are meant only to enhance—never detract.

When you gather as a family to celebrate a birthday or anniversary or just to have Sunday dinner together, an appropriate centerpiece on the dining table and perhaps a family activity before or after the meal often add to the ambiance of the celebration. Although the important thing is the gathering, and the sharing of a meal, those little extras that lend "atmosphere" sometimes help all to appreciate and remember the joy and fellowship of the occasion.

As in our earlier book for cycle C, some of the decorations described have been used either in my parish or my sister's parish; others we have heard about or have seen when visiting other parishes or when on vacation in other cities. Each Sunday or feast day is set up in simple sections:

Inspiration—A brief selection from the readings of the day to suggest a decoration theme. In reflecting on the readings, you may find a different passage that suggests a different theme and decoration.

Decoration—Possibilities for carrying out the theme with a decoration in front of or near the altar, plus extras that might be used in other areas of the church.

Celebration—A parish activity that can be planned to tie in with the theme of the day.

Reflection—A thought that could be read before Mass, or printed (in whole or in part) in the bulletin, or used as a springboard for the homily.

We hope this easy-to-follow format will help you find ways to incorporate ordinary, everyday objects into your altar decorations, just as Jesus used ordinary, everyday examples in his parables.

Depending on the architecture of your church, you may wish to place decorations on a low table in front of the altar, hang them from the ceiling, put them on a wall behind the altar, place them above or between windows or even above the doors at the rear of the church or in the vestibule. It all depends on the type of church building, the type of congregation, and of course, on your imagination! When in doubt, keep it simple, keep it reverent, and never ever let it be so overwhelming that it could detract from the altar or the celebration of the Word made Flesh.

In her book, *Female and Catholic*, Marie McIntyre says, "How do we really worship God—with symbol systems that were better understood in another era and for another people? With references to biblical truths and events that are not part of the common heritage of the people gathered to listen? With symbols that are not explained...?"

As you go through this book, perhaps you will find ways to better explain the symbols and biblical truths to the people of your parish each week so that they will leave the Mass filled with the message of the Scripture readings of the day, filled with a hope or a challenge, a resolve or a reassurance, a new insight or a new awareness of God's love.

FIRST SUNDAY OF ADVENT

Isaiah 2, 1-5
Romans 13, 11-14
Matthew 24, 37-44

You know the time in which we are living. It is now the hour for you to wake from sleep, for our salvation is closer than when we first accepted the faith. The night is far spent; the day draws near. Let us cast off deeds of darkness and put on the armor of light.

Decoration
As always on the first Sunday of Advent, the focal point will probably be an Advent wreath. In addition, place a low table in front of the altar and cover it with a white cloth. Atop the cloth, on the left side, add one long slash of violet-colored satin ribbon or fabric—to extend across the table and hang to the end of the cloth. Atop the satin, place one lighted candle in a pretty brass or glass candle holder and possibly surround it with ivy or greenery. On the wall behind the altar or to one side, hang one long piece of violet-colored satin fabric. (You will add additional strips of deeper purple and one of pink on the other Sundays of Advent.)

Addition
Make a "windsock" of strips of weather-proof material. Use several shades of purple plus one strip of pink. Hang this somewhere on the *outside* of the church—from a light post or sign or above the front door. Depending on the physical layout of your church, you may even want to make several of these and hang one on each side of the door or in a row along the parking lot— just be sure to display the windsock(s) in a place where the breeze will catch the streamers and make them flutter. This will announce to those approaching the building (or passing by during the week) that the church is now celebrating the season of Advent.

Celebration
Using pink or purple paper if possible, photocopy enough

copies of the Advent wreath prayers so that each family can take home a copy. Perhaps you would like to make up prayers appropriate for your parish. If not, you could use this:

Advent Wreath Blessing
Oh God, by whose word all things are sanctified, pour forth thy blessings upon this wreath, and grant that we who use it may prepare our hearts for the coming of Christ and may receive from thee abundant graces. Through Christ our Lord. Amen.

Prayers—to be said before the evening meal each night during Advent.

First Week *(light one purple candle)*
Oh Lord, stir up thy might, we beg thee, and come, that by thy protection we may deserve to be rescued from the threatening dangers of our sins and saved by thy deliverance. Through Christ our Lord. Amen.

Second Week *(light two purple candles)*
Oh Lord, stir up our hearts that we may prepare for thy only begotten son, that through his coming we may be made worthy to serve thee with pure minds. Through Christ our Lord. Amen.

Third Week *(light two purple candles and the pink candle)*
Oh Lord, we beg thee, incline thy ear to our prayers and enlighten the darkness of our minds by the grace of thy visitation. Through Christ our Lord. Amen.

Fourth Week *(light all four candles)*
Oh Lord, stir up thy power, we pray thee, and come; and with great might help us, that with the help of thy grace, thy merciful forgiveness may hasten what our sins impede. Through Christ our Lord. Amen.

Relection
Today we are reminded that it is time to wake from our sleep, to cast off the deeds of darkness and put on the armor of light. We begin by lighting the first candle of our Advent wreath. Per-

haps you would like to bring this custom into your own home by making your own family Advent wreath. Simply make a circle of greenery to symbolize the fact that God is everlasting—with no beginning and no end. Add four candles for the four weeks of Advent and say a little prayer as you light candles each evening before dinner. You will find copies of the Advent wreath prayers at the back of church and we invite you to take home a copy today. As you say the prayer and light the candle each evening this week, discuss how you and your family could do something different during this Christmas season, something that would help you "cast off the deeds of darkness" in today's sinful world and put on the beautiful armor of God's holy light.

SECOND SUNDAY OF ADVENT

Isaiah 11, 1-10
Romans 15, 4-9
Matthew 3, 1-12

Not by appearance shall he judge, nor by hearsay shall he decide, But he shall judge the poor with justice, and decide aright for the land's afflicted.

Decoration
Repeat last week's decoration but add a second strip of satin, this time in a deeper shade of purple—both in the altar decoration and the wall hanging. Also add a second lighted candle—possibly in a height just a bit taller than last week's candle.

Celebration
Most parishes plan to "share" in some way at Christmastime—by giving baskets of food or Christmas gifts either to the poor of their own parish or to a poorer parish. Include in your bulletin today the name and phone number of a contact person in your parish so families can call to ask what specific gifts are needed most and to get directions for delivering them.

Reflection
Today's readings remind us that a shoot shall sprout from the stump of Jesse...and that he shall not judge by appearance or decide by hearsay but shall judge the poor with justice. As we await the joyful season of Christmas amidst beautiful decorations and stores laden with rich foods and expensive gifts for giving, we cannot help but think of those who are poorer than we are, those who will be hungry or alone even at Christmastime. This is the time to discuss as a family what you might do to share your Christmas with someone poorer. Perhaps you might decide to *not* send Christmas cards this year and instead give the cost of the cards to the poor. If you think friends would feel neglected, you could send inexpensive postcards with a note explaining why you are not sending cards and perhaps even mentioning that next year you will not even send postcards so you can donate the cost of postage. *Or* perhaps you might agree

ahead of time to give less expensive or fewer gifts this year to all those with whom you exchange presents. Use the money saved to buy a basket of food or one special gift for a poor family. Look in the bulletin today for the name and number where you can call to get instructions about what gifts are most needed this year and where you can deliver them. This will be a good family project to plan and discuss and shop for together. This can be your way to heed the words of John the Baptist in today's gospel when he says, "Reform your lives! The reign of God is at hand" and to remember the herald's voice in the desert that proclaims, "Prepare the way of the Lord, make straight his paths."

Third Sunday of Advent

Isaiah 35, 1-6, 10
James 5, 7-10
Matthew 11, 2-11

Be patient, my brothers, until the coming of the Lord.

Decoration
Again, repeat the decoration of last week but this Sunday, add strips of deep pink to the decoration and to the wall hanging. Also add a third lighted candle.

Celebration
As Christmas draws nearer, the children become impatient, waiting for Santa Claus and the presents he will bring. Since the world often places more emphasis on Santa than on the Christ Child, take the opportunity to tie the two together. Plan a Santa Breakfast at the parish so that parents can bring their children to talk to Santa at church rather than at a department store. Decorate tables in the church hall with Santa boots filled with greenery and candy canes. Serve "store bought" donuts with milk for the children and coffee for the adults. Perhaps high school girls or members of the Mother's Club could wear green or red aprons and work as table servers and a "jolly" parishioner could serve as Santa for the day. But—in addition, have a storyteller.

This should be someone who is comfortable with children, someone who can read and gesture dramatically and make the stories interesting. She or he should dress in some sort of Christmasy outfit and have some "picture books" to show as the stories are told—*but* the stories should be inspirational, *not* about Santa or Rudolph the Reindeer or Frosty the Snowman. There are many beautiful children's books with stories of the Christ Child and Mary and Joseph, angels and shepherds, the journey of the Wise Men, and Christmas legends. (If possible, put the storyteller in a separate room and only let a few children go in at a time to sit on the floor and listen—so that the breakfast noise will not distract from the story.) The storyteller could give each of the children a little Christmas holy card to take home or a little angel to hang on the Christmas tree—something again to draw attention from Santa to the Christ Child.

You might also set up a little altar—again, in a separate area, away from the hustle and bustle—using one of those statues of Santa kneeling at the crib. Put some greenery around the statue and have some vigil lights so that the children can kneel and say a little prayer and light a candle. (Be sure to have an adult stay in this area at all times so there will be no problem with the matches.)

If there would be a problem in having this affair after one of the Sunday Masses, you could have the Santa Breakfast on a Saturday morning but be sure to announce it a couple of weeks in advance on the bulletin so parents can make arrangements to bring their children. It could become an annual tradition!

Reflection

Today's second reading reminds us to "be patient, my brothers, until the coming of the Lord." It isn't easy—especially for the children—to be patient at this time of the year.

As a little break in this time of waiting, we invite everyone to come and share breakfast with Santa in the church hall. There will be donuts and beverages for all. Children can visit with Santa and there will be a storyteller who will tell of Christmas legends and stories.   Advent is a special opportunity to teach children—and adults— the virtue of patience, the necessity in life of waiting and the value of quiet prayer while we are waiting. This week, let us all reflect on the words of today's second reading, "You too, must be patient. Steady your hearts, because the coming of the Lord is at hand. Do not grumble against one another...as your models in suffering hardships *and in patience*, take the prophets who spoke in the name of the Lord."

FOURTH SUNDAY OF ADVENT

Isaiah 7, 10-14
Romans 1, 1-7
Matthew 1, 18-24

The virgin shall be with child and give birth to a son and they shall call him Emmanuel, a name which means, "God is with us."

Decoration

This week you will complete the Advent decoration by adding the final strip of deep, royal purple satin. You will also add the fourth lighted candle.

Celebration

This last Sunday before Christmas would be an appropriate time to present a Christmas tree "blessing," which families could take home and use to start a family tradition of gathering around the tree for a little quiet time of prayer together before or after gift-sharing. Photocopy the blessing on sheets of green paper and distribute them at the doors or in the pews after Mass. If you don't have a favorite blessing, use this one:

Family Christmas Tree Blessing

Leader: Our help is in the name of the Lord.

All: Who has made heaven and earth.
Then shall all the trees of the forest sing for joy before the Lord, for he has come.

Leader: Let the heavens rejoice and the earth exult,
let the sea roar and all the creatures in it,
let the fields exult and all that is in them.
Then let all the trees of the forest shout for joy
before the Lord when he comes to judge the earth.
He will judge the earth with righteousness and the peoples in good faith.
Glory be to the Father, and to the Son,
and to the Holy Spirit.

All: As it was in the beginning,
          is now and ever shall be, world without end. Amen.
          Then shall all the trees of the forest sing for joy
          before the Lord, for he has come.

Reflection

On this, the last Sunday before Christmas, the first reading tells us "the virgin shall be with child, and bear a son, and shall name him Emmanuel." The second reading says, "To all...beloved of God and called to holiness, grace and peace...." And the gospel reminds us that the name Emmanuel means "God is with us." So we have much reason to rejoice. Remember this as you make your last-minute preparations to celebrate the great feast of Christmas. And as you rejoice, why not take a little time out to start a family tradition of gathering together around the Christmas tree for a few minutes of family prayer? At the church doors (in the pews), you'll find copies of a simple Christmas tree "blessing." Please take home a copy and use it as a beginning for a prayer time of thanksgiving that "God is with us."

CHRISTMAS MIDNIGHT MASS

Isaiah 9: 1-6
Titus 2: 11-14
Luke 2: 1-14

(Readings will vary with other Masses of the day but this decoration will be appropriate for all.)

> *The angel said to them: 'You have nothing to fear! I come to proclaim good news to you—tidings of great joy to be shared by the whole people. This day in David's city a savior has been born to you...'*

Decoration
What more could you need than a beautiful Nativity scene for this season's decoration? Place it below and in front of the altar with a bit of greenery or straw as a background. You might want

to add a Christmas tree to one side but decorate it simply with strands of white lights and possibly a red velvet bow at the top. Behind the altar, on the wall, hang two large banners made of a

---

bright red fabric. Make designs of bright, golden cloth—on one, put a large shimmering star; on the other, the outline or silhouette of the city of David.

Addition—Repeat this design of the city with the star shining above it on your bulletin covers. Possibly add swags of greenery on the side walls of the church and/or wreaths with white lights and red velvet bows.

Celebration

This feast is celebration enough but perhaps you could get some inexpensive Nativity scenes (you can usually find some—made of shiny cardboard—in religious goods stores and they are fairly inexpensive when you buy in volume) and put them in baskets and distribute them to the children after each Mass.

Reflection

Today's decoration and the readings remind us of the great light that shone in the sky to proclaim the good news—while most of those in the city below slept. All too often, in our own lives, God proclaims good news but we continue sleeping, snug in our cities and too involved in our work and worry to look up and see the great light that shines in the darkness. In this shining season of Christmas, let us remember that the angel said, "You have nothing to fear." Let us look up...and see the light... and let it fill our hearts...so that when others look at us, they too will see the light shining forth to proclaim the Good News.

HOLY FAMILY SUNDAY

Sirach 3: 2-6, 12-14
Colossians 3: 12-21
Matthew 2: 13-15, 19-23

Joseph got up and took the child and his mother and left that night for Egypt....He got up, took the child and his mother, and returned to the land of Israel.

Decoration

The beautiful Nativity scene will still be in place today and what better decoration could you have for Holy Family Sunday? You might consider one addition—which you could put in the vestibule or along the sides of the Church. If you have a parish directory, you have available pictures of many of the families of the parish. You could mount some of these (or any photographs you have available from parish activities) on posterboards with the headline "On Holy Family Sunday, we salute the families of our parish!"

Celebration

Since today's readings mention the Holy Family's traveling to Egypt and then back to Israel, how about chartering a bus for a family field trip? And where would you go? Well, if there's a Holy Family parish in your area, perhaps you could plan to go there to share a donut and coffee brunch or a hamburger lunch (ordered in from a fast-food restaurant) with their parishioners and take a tour of their church. Or—many areas now have elaborately lighted outdoor Christmas displays so if there's one nearby, you could visit it and come back to the parish hall for a pizza supper (again ordered in so no one would have to work after all the Christmas cooking!) If the chartered bus would be too expensive, you could "caravan" by handing out maps of where you are going and have families follow along in their own cars. It might be an easy and fun outing in this holiday week.

Reflection

In the readings for today, Holy Family Sunday, parents and children are told to honor each other. And in the Gospel, we hear about the angel who told Joseph to take his family and go to Egypt. Joseph did not question or complain or ask if he could wait until next Tuesday. Joseph took Jesus and Mary and left *that night* to travel over difficult roads that would lead them to a new and foreign land. On this feast of the Holy Family, let us pray that we may be able to follow Joseph's example in trying always to go where God asks us to go and to follow his commands without asking why, without whining or complaining, without dragging our feet and begging, "not yet, Lord, not yet."

OCTAVE OF CHRISTMAS
Solemnity of Mary

Numbers 6: 22-27
Galatians 4: 4-7
Luke 2: 16-21

God sent forth his Son born of a woman...to deliver from the law those who were subjected to it, so that we might receive status as adopted sons. ...You are no longer a slave but a son!

Decoration

Again, the Christmas decorations will still be in place today. To honor the Solemnity of Mary, place at her altar a large box wrapped in white paper with these words printed in big black letters: *"resolution box."* And/or have a pretty basket or bowl filled with strips of white ribbon.

Celebration

Since people often make resolutions on New Year's Day, have slips of paper and pencils available (either have them in the pews or pass them out). Ask parishioners to think of a difficulty or problem in their lives that they need most to "accept." Invite them to write this down on a slip of paper and then come to Mary's altar and put it in the Resolution Box and/or take a slip of the white ribbon (symbolizing Mary's purity and acceptance) and tie it on the Christmas tree (if there is one included in the altar decorations) to make a parish Acceptance Tree.

Reflection

Today, on the first day of this New Year, we celebrate the feast of the Solemnity of Mary. In the first reading, we hear that "God sent forth his Son born of a woman...to deliver from the law those who were subjected to it so that we might receive our status as adopted sons." Mary *accepted* her role in God's plan to bring us salvation. Acceptance was the hallmark of her life—an example, a guide for all of us to follow. The New Year has always been a time to look more closely at your life and think of some way to improve it. Look today and see what difficulty or problem you find most difficult to *accept* in your life. Resolve to ask Mary to help you learn the virtue of acceptance this year. There are slips of paper and pencils available and perhaps you would like to start this new year by writing down your resolution and dropping it in the Resolution Box at Mary's altar. You will also find a basket (bowl) at Mary's altar. It contains slips of white ribbon to symbolize Mary's purity and acceptance. We invite you to take one of these ribbons and tie it on a branch of the tree that is on the altar so that we can turn our parish Christmas tree into an Acceptance Tree for the New Year.

EPIPHANY

Isaiah 60: 1-6
Ephesians 3: 2-3, 5-6
Matthew 2: 1-12

Astrologers from the east arrived one day in Jerusalem inquiring, "Where is the newborn King of the Jews?"...The star which they had observed at its rising went ahead of them until it came to a standstill over the place where the child was....They found the child with Mary his mother. They prostrated themselves and did him homage.

Decoration
Again, the Christmas decorations will still be in place but today you want to call special attention to the three kings. If possible, set them apart from the rest of the Nativity scene and add one or two spotlights that will shine on them and focus attention on them. Ask three parish children to dress as the Kings—wearing crowns and long robes. Have them bring up the offertory gifts and then go to the Nativity scene and "prostrate" themselves for a moment.

Celebration
Invite everyone to come to the parish hall after Mass to share "bean cakes!" Make three cakes for the three kings and if possible, decorate them with "jewels" of gumdrops in a crown design. Put a small "bean" in the batter of each cake before it is baked. The three people who get a piece of cake with a bean in it will be proclaimed "kings for the day" and should be crowned with crowns made of gold or silver foil. Perhaps you might even wish to present them each with a small gift—possibly a paperback edition of the Good News Bible or some other religious item wrapped in gold or silver paper. Or you could give them each a bag of gold-covered chocolate "coins!"

Reflection
Today's gospel tells us that when the astrologers from the east followed the star to find the newborn king of the Jews, they prostrated themselves and did him homage. Today, as we celebrate

the feast of the Epiphany, we too should prostrate ourselves in thanksgiving and petition. We should bow low and thank God for sending us a savior and ask help in following his star to salvation.

To celebrate this feast of the Kings, we invite you to come to the church hall after Mass to share "bean cake" and coffee. There are three cakes to honor the three kings and in each cake, there is a hidden "bean." If you get a piece of cake with a bean in it, you will be one of our three Kings for the day!

BAPTISM OF THE LORD

Isaiah 42: 1-4, 6-7
Acts 10: 34-38
Matthew 3: 13-17

Jesus...appeared before John at the Jordan to be baptized by him. ...After Jesus was baptized...the sky opened and he saw the Spirit of God descend like a dove and hover over him.

Decoration
Today the theme of water would certainly be appropriate so perhaps you could go to a garden supply store and ask to borrow a small fountain with a water pump. Place it in front of and below the altar and surround it with greenery. If this is not possible, place a low table before the altar and cover it with a bright blue cloth (to symbolize the River Jordan), then place a large crystal bowl filled with water in the center of it. Lay one branch of greenery to each side.

Addition—One banner with the design of a flowing river, another with the design of a baptismal font.

Celebration
To call attention to the meaning of this feast, ask the pastor to have the parishioners repeat their baptismal vows today. And/ or ask the priest to go down the aisles, blessing the parishioners with holy water. Perhaps he could use a clear container of water and a green branch—similar to the one in the altar decoration.

Reflection
Today, as we celebrate the feast of the Baptism of the Lord, the gospel reminds us that John protested, saying to Jesus, "I should be baptized by *you*, yet you come to me!" But Jesus told John to "give in," explaining "we must do this if we would fulfill all of God's demands." John gives in. Jesus is baptized. And a voice from the heavens proclaims, "This is my beloved son." How often we too protest something in our lives that seems inappropriate. And God waits for us to "give in." Today, as we repeat our own baptismal vows, we are reminded to reject sin, to affirm faith. We, as John did, must learn to "give in," to accept God's laws and commands so that, in return, we may receive God's peace.

SECOND SUNDAY IN ORDINARY TIME

Isaiah 49: 3. 5-6
1 Corinthians 1: 1-3
John 1: 29-34

*I confess I did not recognize him, though the very reason I
came baptizing with water was that he might be revealed to
Israel.*

Decoration

Today's decoration should include one or more beautiful
masks—not the type you think of in connection with Halloween
but the kind that you might see in a Mardi Gras parade. Many
stores and catalogues now feature them as decorations. Some
are made of enamel or china to use as wall hangings, some are
trimmed with sequins and feathers. Use a background in a solid
color that will serve as a good backdrop for whatever mask you
choose and possibly add a bit of greenery. If you cannot find
masks, you could make some, using heavy posterboard and water colors, and add sequins or sprinkled-on glitter. Or, instead of
any decoration, you could have only two banners with the mask
designs.

Celebration

Have you ever heard of a "shut-ins" program? If there is one
in your city, this would be a good Sunday to list a name and
number in your bulletin where parishioners can call to volunteer
to help in this wonderful work. If your area does *not* have such a
program, ask for volunteers to form a committee to make plans
to start one. The program sponsors a day-away "retreat" one
Saturday each month for people who normally are shut-in and
seldom have an opportunity to get out and socialize. It is usually
held in a meeting room at a hospital so that wheel chairs, ramps,
etc., are available to make it more accessible. The day includes
Mass, lunch, entertainment, two homilies or talks, confession,
and the rosary. Volunteers often say they get as much spiritual
refreshment from this day as the shut-ins do. For information
about setting up such a program, write Noreen Faron, 1192-H
Schulte Hill Rd., Maryland Heights, MO 63043. Or call her at
314-878-0652 in the evening or on weekends.

Reflection

In today's gospel, John speaks of Jesus and says, "I confess I did not *recognize* him, though the very reason I came baptizing with water was that he might be revealed to Israel." How often Jesus appears in our own lives and we do not recognize him. Today's altar decoration reminds you to think of how often you look at others and fail to see Christ in them because you see only the mask they are wearing. Perhaps others look at you and see only the mask *you* are wearing. Are you interested only in outer beauty and fail to see and appreciate inner beauty? When you look at the homeless, the handicapped, the suffering, do you see Jesus? When you look at your own life, do you accept and welcome Jesus in times of hurt as well as happiness? Today we invite you to see and recognize Jesus in others by volunteering to help with the "shut-in" program. For more information, see today's bulletin.

THIRD SUNDAY IN ORDINARY TIME

Isaiah 8: 23, 9: 3
1 Corinthians 1: 10-13. 17
Matthew 4: 12-23 or 4: 12-17

I have been informed...that you are quarreling among your-
selves....Has Christ, then, been divided into parts?

Decoration
Find a large beautiful picture of Jesus. Then take a magic
marker and draw uneven "dividing" lines on it like you might
do to divide it into a jigsaw puzzle. But—don't use too many
lines; just make four or five divisions. And make the lines very
broad and dark so it will be apparent even from a back pew.
Place this in front of and below the altar with an arrangement of
greenery or flowers on each side.

Addition—Banner in some bright color with only a deep gash
of black cutting a zigzag pattern across it to indicate "division."

Celebration
Invite everyone to stay after Mass for a brief prayer service—
to pray for Christian unity. Or have Benediction after Mass and
incorporate prayers for unity. Or write special intentions to add
to today's Intercessions, praying for unity within the parish and
within the church.

Reflection
In today's second reading, we hear the plea, "I beg you...to
agree in what you say. Let there be no factions; rather be united
in mind and judgment." The Corinthians of that day had evi-
dently been arguing among themselves...some saying "I belong
to Paul"...others claiming allegiance to Apollo or Cephas. And
they are asked, "Has Christ then been divided into parts?" Our
altar decoration today reminds us, as does the reading, that we
should *not* argue among ourselves—that we should not choose
up sides, separate into factions, allow bitterness and anger and
hatred to enter our hearts, which should be filled instead with
Christian charity. We should not divide Christ's mystical body.
As a parish, as a nation, as a world-wide church and body of

Christians, we should strive for peace and harmony and Christian love for one another. Let us pray today and every day that we will learn to help and share and care for each other so that no one will ever hear Christians quarreling among ourselves and ask, "Has Christ then been divided into parts?"

We invite you to stay after Mass today to join in a prayer service (or Benediction) to pray for Christian unity and for unity within our own families and our own parish.

Fourth Sunday in Ordinary Time

Zephaniah 2: 3; 3: 12-13
1 Corinthians 1: 26-31
Matthew 5: 1-12

When Christ saw the crowds, he went up on the mountain-side. After he had sat down, his disciples gathered around him, and he began to teach them.

Decoration

Since today's gospel centers on the Beatitudes—or the BE Attitudes, perhaps you might like to just have a long, low flower arrangement on the floor in front of the altar and then place above it, a large, hovering Bee (made with posterboard and watercolors). Or simply letter a large placard with the Beatitudes—taking them exactly from the gospel reading or using a shortened version (see below in Celebration). On this placard, use the headline, "The BE-Attitudes." Hang it behind the altar or by the lectern or in some prominent place.

Celebration

Go to an Instant-Print shop and have small cards printed with the Beatitudes. Give these out at the doors before or after all the Masses. You can use the wording in today's gospel reading or this shortened version:

THE "BE-ATTITUDES"

Blessed are those who need God.
Blessed are those with self-control.
Blessed are those who are sorry for sin.
Blessed are those who hunger and thirst for holiness.
Blessed are the merciful.
Blessed are those who love with all their heart.
Blessed are the peacemakers.
Blessed are those who suffer for doing what is right.

Reflection

In today's gospel reading, we see Jesus going up on the mountainside and sitting down with his disciples gathered around him. We can imagine what it must have been like to sit at the feet of Jesus and listen to him teaching. And the lesson he taught this day was a simple, yet profound one. He gave us the Beatitudes. Today, some people refer to these as the Be-Attitudes—a few simple guidelines to help us Be positive and develop a Christian attitude. Be merciful, be a peacemaker, be holy, be happy in God's love. Think today what you could do to get rid of negative thoughts that distance you from God. Pray for God to help you to be more positive, more trusting, more concerned about others, more holy. Pray that today you will begin to change your life by developing a Be-Attitude!

FIFTH SUNDAY IN ORDINARY TIME

Isaiah 58: 7-10
1 Corinthians 2: 1-5
Matthew 5: 13-1;6

You are the salt of the earth. ...You are the light of the world.

Decoration

Focus the decoration today on salt and light. Use small, large or any size salt shakers plus a box of salt with the label showing. For light—use a coal-oil lamp lighted, a hurricane lamp with a lighted candle in it, several pretty candlesticks with lighted candles or an assortment of lighted vigil lights. You might add a bit of greenery or put a small arrangement of flowers in the middle with the "salts" on one side and the "lights" on the other.

Addition—Banner with the symbolism of a bushel tilted up to show the light shining from under it.

Celebration

Let today be "Talent Sunday." Use this opportunity to find out if anyone in the parish has a "talent" they would be willing to share. Pass out photocopied sheets to all and ask that they fill them out. Then have a bushel basket by the altar or on a side altar or by the back door and ask parishioners to drop their talent sheets in the basket. You will want to make up the "talent sheet" according to the needs and the possibilities in your parish but you could use something like this:

This is don't-hide-your-light-under-a-bushel Sunday!
Do you have any "talents," hobbies, interests or teaching skills that you would be willing to share with others in our parish?

Today's gospel tells us "you are the salt of the earth...the light of the world...your light must shine before men so that they may see goodness in your acts and give praise to your heavenly Father." Following the teaching of this gospel, don't hide your light under a bushel basket—share it with the rest of us. Please fill out this form and drop it in the bushel basket at the back of church (on the side altar).

What are your hobbies? ___quilting ___crafts ___woodworking
___art ___auto repair ___sewing? What else?

Would you be willing to share your time by ___ helping clean
the church, ___ cooking for the priests on the housekeeper's day
off, ____ helping out in the school cafeteria or on the play-
ground, ___ giving a talk about your hobby to the school children, ___ teaching PSR classes, ___ making casseroles to take to
a poor parish, ___ giving rides to the elderly or handicapped,
___ making parish phone calls, ___ organizing a prayer chain,
___ joining a Catholic study group, ___ helping with the liturgy
committee, ___ doing any kind of odd jobs parish committees
might need, (stuffing envelopes, photocopying, setting up tables,
etc.) What else? _____ Do you
have any suggestion for a new parish activity or organization
which might help us share our talents?_____
Name _____ Address _____
Phone number _____ I am available to help in the ___
daytime ___ evening ___ either.

Reflection

Today is Parish Talent Sunday! The altar decoration symbolizes the words in today's gospel—"You are the salt of the earth,
you are the light of the world." The gospel also tells us that you
do not light a lamp and then hide it under a bushel basket. Instead, "your light must shine before men so they may see the
goodness in your acts and give praise to your heavenly Father."
So what are *your* talents? Have you been hiding your light under a bushel basket? You don't have to have a special, newswor-
thy talent—maybe you could help cut the grass in the summer,
dish out food in the school cafeteria, stuff envelopes for parish
mailings *or* maybe you know how to do crafts or carpentry work
and could teach others how to do this. No matter whether you
are young or old or in-between—we all have talents that we
could use to help the parish. So take one of the talent sheets today and fill it out and drop it in the bushel basket. And never
forget the words of today's gospel....you are the salt of the earth,
the light of the world.

Sixth Sunday in Ordinary Time

Sirach 15: 15-20
1 Corinthians 2: 6-10
Matthew 5: 17-37 or 5: 20-22, 27-28, 33-34, 37

Do not think I have come to abolish the law and the prophets. I have come, not to abolish them, but to fulfill them.

Decoration
Since today's gospel is about the "law," perhaps the decoration could be only a policeman's hat, badge and handcuffs placed on a small table covered with a white or red cloth. Or simply an arrangement of greenery centered with a judge's gavel.

Addition—Banners with the symbolism of the scales of justice.

Celebration
Put a table in the vestibule with a "suggestion box," slips of paper and pencils. You can make the box simply by covering a box with a solid-colored paper and lettering "suggestion box" in prominent letters. Then cut a large enough slit in the top so it will be easy to insert the slips of paper. If you get enough response from this, you might consider keeping the box in the vestibule for several weeks to see if you will continue to get suggestions.

Reflection
Today's gospel speaks sternly of the law. Jesus reminds us, "Do not think I have come to *abolish* the law and the prophets. I have come, *not* to abolish them, but to fulfill them." Our altar decoration reminds us that we must obey the laws of God and the laws of the land. But, in order to do this, we must "police" ourselves. Today's easy-going, lawless society makes it very easy for even good Christians to become lax, to take liberties with the law, to make excuses for overlooking or getting around the law. In the same way, sometimes it is necessary to "police" our own parish. Perhaps we have become lax in some areas where we should be more alert. Is there something in the parish that *you* think should be changed—or stopped—or started?

In order to improve, we must first be aware of what *needs* improvement so today we ask you to help us "police the parish!" You'll find a Suggestion Box in the vestibule. Please take a few minutes after Mass to write down any suggestions you have and drop them in the box. And for the rest of this week—and for the rest of your life—remember Jesus' words in today's gospel, "I have come *not* to abolish the law but to fulfill it."

First Sunday of Lent

Genesis 2: 7-9; 3: 1-7
Romans 5: 12-19 or 5: 12, 17-19
Matthew 4: 1-11

Jesus was led into the desert by the Spirit to be tempted by the devil. He fasted forty days and forty nights.

Decoration
To indicate the "desert" of Lent, use several pots of various types of cactus. You should include at least one or two of the very tall varieties so they will make a stark display. If you must use smaller varieties, place them on slabs of wood or large rocks at various heights so there will be dimension to the display. Set these in front of but to one side of the altar. Add more large rocks around the base of the pots.

Addition—purple banner with "40" in black, another purple banner with the design of a loaf of bread and some stones.

Celebration
In some areas, the first Sunday of Lent is observed with the rite of the "Enrollment of Names" where catechumens write down their names as candidates to be baptized at the Easter Vigil. In keeping with this, you could have a parish prayer vigil or a Holy Hour on this Sunday night to pray for all catechumens—of your parish, your city, the world. Or—you could ask the pastor to read out the names of all the catechumens in your parish and ask the parishioners to pray especially for them during this lenten season.

Reflection
In today's gospel, Jesus is led into the desert to fast for forty days and forty nights. Our altar decoration reminds us that we too have begun our journey into the lenten desert of fast and penance. We recall how the tempter tried to taunt Jesus into turning rocks into bread and we know that Jesus can understand when we too are tempted in today's tempestuous world. As you pray to persevere this Lent, to endure the desert so that you can rejoice with the risen Lord at Easter, we ask you to also pray for

this year's catechumens who have been studying and preparing so that they too may know new life through their baptism into the church at the Easter Vigil.

Please read the notice in today's bulletin about next Sunday's Hardship Supper. If you would like to attend, please put your name on the sign-up sheet in the vestibule today. (Bulletin Notice: Next Sunday evening at 6 P.M., we will have a Hardship Supper of only bread and soup. There will be no charge but all donations will go to help the poor and homeless. The Supper will be followed by Stations of the Cross at 7 P.M.)

SECOND SUNDAY OF LENT

Genesis 12: 1-4 2
Timothy 1: 8-10
Matthew 17: 1-9

Bear your share of the hardship which the gospel entails.

Decoration

Perhaps you would like to continue the cactus decoration on the altar all during the lenten season. If not, today, to tie in with the Hardship Supper, have a small table covered with a purple cloth. Make a "place setting" with a place mat, a plate, a clear glass of water, a large soup spoon and a napkin. Have a covered soup tureen or covered casserole dish on one side and on the other, a tray with a loaf of unsliced bread.

Celebration

Last Sunday's sign-up sheet will have given you an idea of how many to expect for today's Hardship Supper. Ask different ladies of the parish to bring pots of soup—if you do not have kitchen facilities, you could ask that they bring the soup in "crock pots" that can be plugged into any electric outlet. Serve only the soup, bread and glasses of water. You might add juice for the children and coffee or tea for adults—but not soft drinks or dessert. It should be a true Hardship meal. Have "homeless" baskets or boxes for donations on the tables or at the door and give whatever you collect to the St. Vincent de Paul Society or whatever parish group you have to help the poor. After the meal, all can go to the church for a prayer-time with the Stations of the Cross.

Reflection

In today's second reading, we are reminded to "bear your share of the hardship which the gospel entails." In keeping with this instruction, we invite all parishioners to come this evening to a Hardship Supper in the church hall. As our altar decoration suggests, we will share only soup and bread. There will be no charge but we ask for donations so that we can sacrifice what we might have spent on this evening's meal and give that money to the poor and homeless. If you did *not* sign up last Sunday, please add your name to the sign-up sheet in the vestibule today so that we will know how many to expect. The supper will be served at 6 P.M., followed by Stations of the Cross at 7 P.M. By sharing this hardship supper together, we can rejoice in the other words in today's second reading, "God has saved us and has called us to a holy life."

Third Sunday of Lent

Exodus 17: 3-7
Romans 5: 1-2, 5-8
John 4: 5-42 or 4: 5-15, 19-26, 39, 40-42

Whoever drinks the water I give him will never be thirsty.

Decoration

If you have chosen to keep the cactus arrangement, that will be sufficient for today. If not, use a small table with a purple cloth and add a large rock and a "staff" or long heavy walking stick.

Addition—one banner with the design of water pouring from a rock, another banner with the design of a water jar tipped with water flowing from it.

Celebration

Go to a garden supply store and buy bags of medium-sized rocks like those used in landscaping—not small pebbles but rocks about the size of a small egg. Put these in some kind of containers—baskets or buckets that will not be too heavy to hold. Ask the parish Boy Scouts or Girl Scouts or school children to stand at the church doors and give a rock to each person as they leave the church.

The Scrutinies

If you have many catechumens in your parish, you may wish to observe the custom of "scrutiny." After the liturgy of the Word, on the Third, Fourth and Fifth Sundays of Lent, the catechumens are called to come before the community. All present pray in silence for the catechumens and then join in intercessions for them.

The presider lays hands on each of the elect and prays that they will be delivered from the power of evil and become witnesses to the gospel. A song may be sung. Then the catechumens are dismissed and the faithful continue with the liturgy of the eucharist.

Reflection

As we journey through the desert of Lent, today's readings

speak to us of water. In the gospel, we see Jesus with the woman at the well and in the first reading, we hear God telling Moses that he should strike a rock with his staff and water will pour forth. Today, after Mass, there will be children at each of the church doors to give you a rock—yes, a plain ordinary rock. Carry this with you through the remaining days of Lent as a reminder that even when things get rocky, you can rely on God's cleansing water of baptism for refreshment and redemption.

FOURTH SUNDAY OF LENT

1 Samuel 16: 1, 6-7, 10-13
Ephesians 5: 8-14
John 9: 1-41 or 9: 1, 6-9, 13-17, 34-38

Awake, O sleeper, arise from the dead, and Christ will give you light.

Decoration
Again, you may be continuing the cactus decoration. If not, simply use a table with a purple cloth and in the center of it, place an alarm clock and a lighted candle. Add a bit of greenery on each side.

Addition—one or more banners using the symbols of a clock, an eye and a light.

Celebration
Have a "quiet time" after the eucharist and ask people to use this time to recall their lenten resolutions and consider how well they have kept them and then to determine what they can do for the remaining days of Lent to "awake" and receive the light.

Second Scrutiny (see third Sunday of Lent)

Reflection
Today's Gospel tells of the blind man whose eyes are opened by Jesus and the first reading reminds us, "Awake, O sleeper, arise from the dead, and Christ will give you light." On this fourth Sunday of Lent, we ask you to spend a few quiet minutes after you receive the eucharist to consider whether your eyes have been opened during this Lent. What were your lenten resolutions on Ash Wednesday and how well have you kept them? Even if you have faltered, it is not too late to awake and arise and renew your lenten promises so that you will be ready to share in the glorious light of Easter.

FIFTH SUNDAY OF LENT

Ezekiel 37:12-14
Romans 8: 8-11
John 11: 1-45 or 11: 3-7, 17, 20-27, 33-45

I will open your graves and have you rise from them.

Decoration
If you have continued the cactus arrangement, that will be sufficient. If not, simply put a black cloth on the small table and add a few strips of white linen to symbolize the linen strips with which Lazarus was bound.

Celebration
Since death is mentioned in each of the readings, it would be an appropriate time to pray for the dead of the parish. Perhaps you could read a list of those who have died in the past year and have the assembly answer, "May their souls and the souls of the faithful departed, through the mercy of God, rest in peace. Amen."

Third Scrutiny (see Third Sunday of Lent)

Reflection
Each of the three readings today remind us of death. The gospel tells of Jesus commanding Lazarus to "come out" from the tomb. In the first reading, we hear, "I will open your graves and have you rise from them..." and the second reading tells us, "If the Spirit of him who raised Jesus from the dead dwells in you, then he who raised Christ from the dead will bring your mortal bodies to life also through his Spirit dwelling in you." In this fifth week of Lent, let us remember to pray for the dead—especially for those in your own family who have died and also for those in our parish family. And, as we draw closer to the sad days of Holy Week climaxed by the joyous celebration of the resurrection of our Lord, let us rejoice that we have been given the promise that we too shall rise from the dead as Jesus did!

PASSION SUNDAY
(Palm Sunday)

Isaiah 50: 4-7
Philippians 2: 6-11
Matthew 26: 14-27, 66 or 27: 11-54

Tell the daughter of Zion, your King comes to you without display riding an ass, astride a colt, the foal of a beast of burden.

Decoration
Do you remember where you stored the Nativity scene from last Christmas? If you do, find the statue of the donkey. If your parish does not have a fairly large donkey statue, perhaps you could borrow one from a neighboring parish or from a religious goods store. Place this statue on the floor in front of altar. To one side, lay a piece of burlap or coarse-weave cloth to symbolize the cloaks which were placed on the donkey in the Scripture passage. On the other side, lay quite a few branches of palm and let the palm branches come out to the front of the altar to form a sort of "path." (If your donkey is not large enough to make a dramatic arrangement, you may need to place it on a low bench which is covered with the burlap and then place the palms accordingly.)

Addition—Attach some palm branches plus purple streamers (strips of purple ribbon or crepe paper) to the top of tall poles. Ask altar boys or ushers to hold these aloft as they lead in the Procession of Palms. These poles could be placed at each side of the altar and remain as part of the decoration until Good Friday.

Celebration
Today, the only celebration you will need is the procession of palms plus the reading of the passion narrative.

Reflection
In today's competitive world, we have often seen the news media proclaim someone a hero one week and then speak of that same person as a villain the following week. We've seen sports and entertainment stars, businessmen and politicians, honored

and cheered as celebrities at one time, only to be criticized and ridiculed a short time later. And so we can understand the people of Jerusalem who greeted Jesus with hosannas and palm branches one day and then turned on him and crucified him only a few days later. How easy it is for people of our day also to "follow the crowd," to be influenced by what others say or do. On this Palm Sunday, consider: "Have you been tempted to turn away from Jesus? To follow the crowd to approve of x-rated movies, to live a non-Christian lifestyle, to make excuses for breaking God's commandments because 'everybody else does it?' Consider. Are you one of the ones who crucify Jesus in today's world?"

HOLY THURSDAY

This evening, the only "decoration" you will need will be the jars of water, towels, etc. for the rite of Washing of the Feet. As a "celebration," you might consider having a Parish Seder Meal before the evening liturgy. You can probably find a book at the library which will give you directions for planning this but here is a simple format of what you should include:

* Matzoh crackers or unleavened bread. As this is served, someone can read the Scripture account of the manna given in the desert and/or the unleavened bread made in a hurry during the Exodus.

* Roast lamb served with wine and/or grape juice. As this is served, read the story of how the Israelites were told to slay a lamb and sprinkle the blood on their doorposts.

* Bitter herbs (parsley, horseradish, green onion). Tell of the bitter life of those who are enslaved (both in the Scripture and in our world today).

* A little dish of salt water. Ask those present to dip the parsley into this and taste it, as a reminder of the tears of all who are or have been persecuted for their faith.

* A mixture of chopped apple, nuts, cinnamon and wine. Explain that this symbolizes the bricks which the children of Israel made during their captivity. Remind all that this "Seder meal" symbolizes the supper Jesus shared with his apostles on that blessed night when he gave us the holy eucharist. Have a moment of silent thanksgiving before you leave to go to church for the Mass of the Lord's Supper.

GOOD FRIDAY

In earlier days in the church, the sound of bells and music was replaced this day with the sound of wooden clackers—wooden sticks hit against each other to sound a dull thud. Perhaps you could revive this custom as you sing, "This is the wood of the cross..."

HOLY SATURDAY

The decorations for the Easter vigil will be those for Easter Sunday but perhaps you might like to add this: On Palm Sunday, put a note in the bulletin asking all those who come to this celebration to bring along a small bell.

Make a beautiful white satin banner large enough to cover the crucifix in your church. Center this banner with a brilliant cross made of bright colors and possibly covered with sequins or glitter. Roll this and hang it above the crucifix.

When the Gloria is sung on this night, unfurl the banner so that the shining cross covers the crucifix and as it unfurls, have the altar boys and choir to start ringing bells, summoning all assembled to ring the bells which they have brought from home to join together in a joyful Easter Gloria.

Easter Sunday

Acts 10: 34, 37-43
Colossians 3: 1-4 or
1 Corinthians 5: 6-8
John 20: 1-9

*Be intent on things above rather than things on earth. This
is the day the Lord has made; let us rejoice and be glad.*

Decoration

The mellow, pure white of the traditional Easter lilies is always effective on this day so you might want to include them in
today's decoration but put the main focus behind the altar as a
backdrop for today's glorious celebration. Take strips of glitter-
ing silver or gold fabric and hang these behind the altar, from
ceiling to floor or in graduated lengths—to symbolize the radiant
brilliance of resurrection. You might add some spotlights fo-
cused on this to make it shimmer and glitter even more. If you
have used the banner with the glorious Cross on Holy Saturday,
this will be another focus, possibly in the center of the shimmering strips behind the altar if that is where your church's crucifix
hangs. If you have not used this banner, consider making a
wooden cross and paint it in a bright, springtime color and cover
it with sequins or glued-on "jewels." Put this in a prominent
place and bank the base of it with the Easter lillies or with pots of
colorful tulips or hydrangeas.

Celebration

This day is celebration enough itself but you might consider
buying enough Easter holy cards to pass these out after the
Masses—either to all or only to the children.

Reflection

Today's altar decoration reminds us to rejoice in the glorious
message of this Easter Sunday. Death has been vanquished and
we have been given the shining promise of resurrection and eternal life. Let us rejoice and be glad! The first reading tells us,
"They killed him...only to have God raise him up on the third
day...." And the gospel tells us again of how the stone had been

---

moved away and the burial wrappings were lying on the ground—and the disciple who found this, "saw and believed." Let us too see and believe. Yes, life is real and there will be Good Fridays in all our lives but Jesus has shown us how to survive and rise above them. Jesus has proved to us that we can rise as he did in a glorious resurrection—to find new hope and new life. Let us all ponder this deeply as we join together today in this joyful Easter celebration.

Second Sunday of Easter

Acts 2: 42-47 1
Peter 1: 3-9
John 20: 19-31

Despite the locked doors, Jesus came and stood before them....(He said) to Thomas: "Take your finger and examine my hands. Put your hand into my side. Do not persist in your unbelief, but believe!"

Decoration

You will probably want to keep the lovely Easter decorations for today. But if you wish to do more, you could add the symbolism of the locked room by hanging a mobile made of keys or locks.

Celebration

Since today's Gospel speaks of "doubting Thomas," this would be a good day to introduce the idea of a parish "Question Box." Ask your pastor if he would be willing to occasionally have a Question Box Sunday to answer parishioners' questions. Since it would be too time-consuming to ask for oral questions, put a Question Box in the vestibule so that people can write down their questions and then the pastor can choose the most appropriate ones to answer from the pulpit. To make the container, simply cover a box with paper and use a magic marker to label it as a *question box* and possibly draw on some question marks—???—in various sizes.

Reflection

We can certainly all identify with today's gospel story of the "doubting Thomas." Even though the doors were locked, Jesus came and stood before the disciples and spoke with them but when they told the absent Thomas what had happened, he needed *proof* before he would believe. And so Jesus came back and said, "Examine my hands. Put your hand into my side. Do not persist in your unbelief." We all have doubts at times....we all have questions and wonderments...and sometimes we lock our minds and hearts and refuse to let anyone in—even Jesus. If you have serious doubts, perhaps you should seek the counsel of a Spiritual Adviser, do more spiritual reading or take a refresher course in Catholic doctrine. But, to help answer some of the little "I wonder why..." questions, we have put a Question Box in the vestibule today. Please feel free to write down any of your questions and put them in the box. Then, whenever we have accumulated enough questions, we'll have a Question Box Sunday and the pastor will use the homily time to answer your questions. Until then, let us all open the locks on our minds and hearts and as we seek answers, let us remember Jesus' words to Thomas: "Do not persist in your unbelief, but believe!"

THIRD SUNDAY OF EASTER

Acts 2: 14, 22-28
1 Peter 1: 17-21
Luke 24: 13-35

He...then broke the bread and began to distribute it to them.
With that their eyes were opened and they recognized him.

Decoration
Cover a small table with a nice white cloth that might look like a dinner table cloth. OR use a red-checkered cloth that might look like what you would use on a kitchen table. Find a pretty loaf of unsliced bread. Break it in half and place it on a bread tray or plate in the middle of the table. Add greenery and candles. If this arrangement is not large enough, you could add a basket on each side filled with broken pieces of bread.

Addition—banner with the design of a dusty road (to symbolize the road to Emmaus), another banner with the design of broken bread.

Celebration
What organizations in your parish help the "broken"—the Knights of Columbus, the St. Vincent de Paul Society or...? Ask a representative from one or all such organizations to make a brief presentation from the pulpit today, explaining their work and asking for new members. Have representatives in the vestibule after all the Masses, wearing badges to identify them, ready to hand out literature about the organizations, answer questions and sign up new members.

Reflection
Today the gospel story of the disciples on the road to Emmaus tells us that only when he broke the bread did they recognize him! Today we can all offer prayers of thanksgiving that we, like the disciples, can share in the broken bread of the eucharist. But this is also a good opportunity too to think of the people in our society whose lives are "broken"—physically, emotionally, financially. There are several organizations in our parish who reach out to help these "broken" ones—and they always need

more members, more helping hands, more disciples. Today, representatives from these organizations are here to tell us about their work and to ask if *you* might like to join them. There will be literature and information in the vestibule. Please take time to talk to the representatives. And when you receive the eucharist today, pray about what you can do personally to reach out to the broken—and also what you can do to heal your own brokenness so that you can see and recognize Jesus in your life.

FOURTH SUNDAY OF EASTER

Acts 2: 14, 36-41
1 Peter 2: 20-25
John 10: 1-10

Christ suffered for you in just this way and left you an example, to have you follow in his footsteps.

Decoration

Cut out "footsteps" from brown paper and place them across the sanctuary floor leading to a pair of men's sandals and a walking stick laying on the floor in front of the altar. You might add a bit of greenery by the footsteps to indicate a path or make a "path" of pebbles or artificial grass like Astroturf.

Addition—a banner with the design of footprints or a mobile made of footprints.

Celebration

Make today Sandal Sunday! Everyone's so busy today, they seldom have time to just stop by church for a quiet visit with the Lord. Announce that the church will be open all day so that anyone can just come in and take off their sandals and sit down quietly for a nice, comfortable visit. You may or may not wish to leave the Blessed Sacrament exposed and close the day with Benediction in the evening.

Reflection

Today's readings call us to pause and pay attention. In the first reading, Peter urges, "Save yourself from this generation which has gone astray." In the second reading, we hear, "Christ suffered for you...and left you an example, to have you follow in his footsteps." And in the gospel, Jesus says, "I am the gate. Whoever enters though me will be safe." These readings indicate that we need to walk more closely with Jesus...to follow in his footsteps. But we're all so busy...there's so little time to "enter through the gate where we will be safe." Our altar decoration of the footsteps and sandals announces that today will be Sandal Sunday. Think about how long it's been since you took off your shoes and just sat at the feet of the Lord to listen. Today, the church will be open all afternoon so that you can come in and take off your sandals and just sit and have a quiet, comfortable visit with the Lord. Ask him to show you how to follow in his footsteps...tell him you want to "save yourself from this generation which has gone astray"...ask him to let you into the sheepgate so you will be safe. Take advantage of this Sandal Sunday to take a walk with the Lord.

FIFTH SUNDAY OF EASTER

Acts 6: 1-7
1 Peter 2: 4-9
John 14: 1-12

Come to the Lord, a living stone....you too are living stones, built as an edifice of spirit...a stone which the builders rejected has become the corner stone...

Decoration
How about using a concrete block for today's decoration! You might even want to use several of them, piled haphazardly in front of or to the side of the altar—with a bit of greenery to each side or some green vines wound about the blocks.

Celebration
Since parish organizations are often the "building blocks" of the parish, honor them this Sunday. You might try to enlist new members by talking a bit about various groups and/or listing them in the parish bulletin with names and phone numbers where parishioners could call for more information about joining. Or you could invite the officers of all organizations to come and sit in front of the church at one of the Masses and then have a breakfast/brunch to honor them—either at the parish hall or at an inexpensive restaurant.

Reflection
Today's altar decoration reflects the fact that today's readings speak of building...of building with living stones. In the first reading, the disciples are looking for helpers and we are told the number of the disciples increased enormously. In the gospel, Jesus says, "The man who has faith in me will do the works I do." And the second reading says, "the Lord is a living stone...and you too are living stones, built as an edifice of spirit...you are a chosen race...a people he claims for his own to proclaim (his) glorious works...." Our parish is built of living stones, of workers who continue to do the work of Jesus and proclaim his good news. Today we honor the leaders of our various parish organizations and we invite *all* parishioners to consider joining at least

one parish group so that we can all work together to build up the parish and continue the work of the Lord. We cannot all be leaders but we *can* all be helpers—if you cannot help by working, you can always help by prayer and cooperation. The second reading says the stone can also be an obstacle, a stumbling block...so today let's pray that we will not stumble but instead use the mortar of Christian love to hold together all the living stones in our parish to strengthen and continue the work of our Lord, the cornerstone.

SIXTH SUNDAY OF EASTER

Acts 8: 5-8, 14-17
1 Peter 3: 15-18
John 14: 15-21

A little while now and the world will see me no more; but you see me as one who has life, and you will have life.

Decoration
Make one or more large puffy "clouds" of white nylon net. Then, depending on whether you have electric outlets available, put an electric light or a battery-powered flashlight inside the poufs so that the light will shine through. If physically feasible, you could even suspend these from the ceiling or put them on a back wall behind the altar. (*Note:* This decoration will also be appropriate for the feast of the Ascension this week.)

Celebration
Rather than a parish activity today, simply ask parishioners to spend some time during the day to consider where they "see" Jesus. You might include a note about this in the bulletin.

Reflection
In today's gospel reading, Jesus is preparing his disciples for his ascension when he tells them, "A little while now and the world will see me no more; but you see me as one who has life, and you will have life. On that day, you will know that I am in my Father, and you in me, and I in you." Today's altar decorations remind us that the world's view is sometimes clouded so that it sees Jesus no more but *we* as Christians should be able to see the light of Jesus shining through the clouds of doubt and worry. This afternoon, spend a little quiet time alone looking for Jesus. Where do *you* see him in the world—in the beauty of sunsets and flowers, in the joy of children's laughter, in your family or friends? Perhaps your view too is sometimes clouded and it is hard to see Jesus in your life. When those times come, remember those other reassuring words in today's gospel when Jesus tells his disciples—and us—"I will not leave you orphaned. I will come back to you."

Seventh Sunday of Easter

Acts 1: 12-14
1 Peter 4: 13-16
John 17: 1-11

I entrusted to them the message you entrusted to me, and they received it...I am in the world no more, but these are in the world as I come to you.

Decoration

Center today's decoration with a large, attractive Bible displayed on a bookstand. On each side, arrange an assortment of various types of Bibles—a children's Bible, a pocket-sized Bible, an illustrated Bible, etc.—or other religious books. Or flank the center Bible with stacks of the New Testaments you plan to make available for sale today. Intersperse the books with sprays of greenery or vines of ivy.

Addition—a banner depicting a Bible with the Message, "Pass On the Good News." Or two banners: one with the design of a Bible and the words, "The Good News"; the second with the words, "Pass It On!"

Celebration

How about having a Pass-it-On Sale today! Contact a publisher or religious supply store to see if you can negotiate a very low price on paperback editions of the New Testament. If this is not successful, perhaps one of the parish organizations could donate money toward the purchase so that you could offer Bibles for one dollar or fifty cents or the lowest price possible. You might also include some other inexpensive religious books and encourage people to buy Bibles or books for themselves—but also to give away in order to pass on the Good News!

Reflection

In today's gospel, Jesus speaks to the Father and says, "I entrusted to them the message you entrusted to me and they received it. ...I am in the world no more but *these* are in the world as I come to you." Jesus entrusted the Good News to his disciples and they passed it on to us. Today we are the ones entrusted ed with the Father's message...we are the ones who must Pass-it-On to others. To help you do this, we are having a Pass-it-On Sale today! You can purchase a paperback edition of the New Testament for only _____! Keep it for yourself so you can study it more frequently and then pass on the Good News to others. OR buy a copy to give away to a friend or relative so that you can pass on the Good News that way. We also have some inexpensive religious books so stop by the vestibule and take advantage of this Pass-It-On Sale! And remember Jesus' words— "I am in the world no more....but I have entrusted *to them* the message you entrusted to me."

PENTECOST SUNDAY

Acts 2: 1-11
1 Corinthians 12: 3-7, 12-13
John 20: 19-23

Suddenly from up in the sky there came a noise like a strong, driving wind which was heard all through the house where they were seated. Tongues as of fire appeared which parted and came to rest on each of them.

Decoration

Make a large mobile today to hang from the ceiling—either in front of or behind or to the side of the altar. (If you usually have a hanging Advent wreath, you could hang it from that same spot.) The design will of course be tongues of fire! To make the flames, use varying shades of red, orange and yellow to simulate the colors in fire. If possible, use plexiglass or a see-through material so the light will catch it as the mobile moves. If not, you could simply use varying colors of heavy posterboard or even use water colors to paint stylized shoots of flame.

Addition—you might want to add a long low arrangement of red flowers in front of the altar.

Celebration

Since Pentecost is the "birthday of the church," invite parishioners to the parish hall for a birthday party. Have red and white balloons for the children. Serve sheet cake decorated like a birthday cake in red and white—plus red punch and coffee. Have a "greeter" who will try to make any newcomers feel welcome.

Reflection

How exciting yet terrifying these days must have been in the early church. First, the disciples were horrified when their leader was crucified. Then they rejoiced in his resurrection. But then he left them again and once more, they were on their own, in fear and trembling. And then a great wind came and tongues of fire! They were filled with the Spirit and were afraid no more. But now it was time for them to go out and make bold proclamations about the Good News! They could no longer keep the story of Jesus to themselves. It was time to share it and make converts and begin a new church. Today, we too must be filled with the Spirit—ready to share our beliefs, evangelize and try to make converts, and continue the church which the early disciples began.

Since many people refer to Pentecost as the "birthday" of the Catholic church, we invite you all to a birthday party today in the parish hall so that we can all rejoice together in the Spirit!

Trinity Sunday

Exodus 34: 4-6, 8-9
2 Corinthians 13: 11-13
John 3: 16-18

All the holy ones send greetings to you. The grace of the Lord Jesus Christ, and the love of God, and the fellowship of the Holy Spirit be with you all!

Decoration
Continue the decoration from last week. *or*—in honor of Trinity Sunday—continue to use the mobile *but* redesign it slightly. Keep some of the flames to represent the Spirit, remove the other flames and replace them with crosses to symbolize the Son, and Eyes of God (the triangle with an eye in it) to symbolize the Father. (Be sure to make the crosses and the Eyes of God of the same material that you used for the flames so the design will be consistent.) Or make banners with designs of the Eye, the cross and the flame.

Celebration
Since today's second reading tells us to "encourage one another and to greet one another with a kiss," suggest that at the Kiss of Peace, parishioners turn to each other and—instead of shaking hands—make the sign of the cross on the forehead of the person next to them, saying "In the name of the Father and of the Son and of the Holy Spirit, peace be with you."

Reflection
Today we celebrate Trinity Sunday and honor the Father, the Son and the Holy Spirit. The first reading tells of how the Father came to speak to Moses on Mount Sinai; the gospel reminds us that the Son came into the world *not* to condemn the world but to save it; and the second reading reflects the Spirit when it asks us to encourage one another. That reading also contains this greeting: "The grace of the Lord Jesus Christ, and the love of God, and the fellowship of the Holy Spirit be with you all!" What a wonderful greeting, what a wonderful blessing—the *grace* of Jesus, the son; the *love* of God, the Father; the *fellowship* of

of the Holy Spirit! In keeping with this idea of greeting—on this Trinity Sunday—we suggest that you extend a special greeting or blessing of your own to your fellow parishioners. At the Kiss of Peace today, instead of just shaking hands, turn to the person next to you and make the sign of the cross on his or her forehead, saying "In the name of the Father and of the Son and of the Holy Spirit—peace be with you."

THE BODY AND BLOOD OF CHRIST
(Corpus Christi)

Deuteronomy 8: 2-3, 14-16
1 Corinthians 10: 16-17
John 6: 51-58

If you do not eat the flesh of the Son of Man and drink his blood, you have no life in you.

Decoration
Put a small table in front of the altar and set it as you would a miniature dinner table. Use a pretty table cloth and a lovely flower centerpiece flanked on each side with candles in silver or crystal candleholders. Put a "place setting" on each end of the table—using fancy china plates, silver knives, forks and spoons, a pretty napkin and a crystal goblet.

Addition—make two banners in a color that will coordinate with the colors of your "dinner table"; on one, use the design of a loaf of bread or a host and on the other, use the design of a goblet or chalice of wine.

Celebration
Since today's second reading mentions "we, many though we are, are one body," wouldn't this be an appropriate time to bridge the generation gap? If there is a teen-age organization in your parish, ask that they host a Continental breakfast—juice, coffee, sweet rolls or donuts—and either invite the "Golden Agers" of the parish or all parish parents and grandparents to be their guests. They might even like to put on some kind of entertainment—sing some Golden Oldie songs or have one act as a disc jockey and play some Golden Oldie records. Encourage the teens to mingle and chat. If there is a family that has been in the parish a long time, the teens might ask one of the "seniors" to tell what the parish was like when he or she was a teen.

Reflection
When you go out to dinner at a fancy restaurant, you are usually seated at a table that looks a bit like our altar decoration today—set with nice china and crystal and silver and maybe with

flowers and candles. It's a special occasion when you share a meal like that. But the *most* special occasion is when we come together to share the eucharistic meal of Jesus' body and blood. Today the church celebrates the feast of Corpus Christi, the body and blood of Christ. In today's gospel, Jesus tells us "if anyone eats this bread, he shall live forever....if you do *not* eat the flesh of the Son of Man and drink his blood, you have no life in you." In many parts of the world today, Catholics are not permitted to attend Mass or there are no priests to say Mass so let us give thanks today that we can come together as a community of God to share the bread that will give us everlasting life.

In honor of this feast and in keeping with the second reading which notes that "we, though many, are one," the teenagers invite all "golden agers," all parents and grandparents, to be their guests for a Bridge-the-Generation-Gap Breakfast!

SEVENTH SUNDAY IN ORDINARY TIME

Leviticus 19: 1-2, 17-18
1 Corinthians 3: 16-23
Matthew 5: 38-48

Love your enemy, pray for your persecutors.

Decoration
Use any pretty, solid-colored cloth. Atop it, make an arrangement of a lot of interesting-looking, different-sized picture frames. But—instead of putting pictures in the frames, put a plain white sheet of paper with a black question mark on it or a sheet of black paper with a white question mark on it. Have one frame with a mirror in it. Use greenery or flowers interspersed among the frames to complete the arrangement.

Celebration
Let this be Love-Your-Enemy Week! Put an announcement in the bulletin something like this: "We challenge you! Can you love your enemy for a whole week? Who *is* your enemy? Maybe you are your *own* worst enemy. Think about that. This week, try to follow the directions in this Sunday's readings: 'Love your neighbor as yourself...Love your enemies, pray for your persecutors...'"

Reflection
Today's readings offer us a difficult lesson. The first tells us to "not bear hatred for your brother...take no revenge and cherish no grudge....love your neighbor as yourself." The second reading reminds us to not be wise in the ways of the world but in the ways of the Spirit. And the gospel says, "Love your enemies, pray for your persecutors." But who *are* your enemies? Our altar decoration suggests that we try to picture our enemies. Do you know who your enemies are? Have you been holding grudges and seeking revenge against the wrong ones? Included in the altar decoration is a mirror. Maybe you should look in the mirror and ask if *you* are your own worst enemy! Think about that this week and try to heed the words of Scripture—let go of past hatreds and open yourself to the spirit of love. Love your enemies and pray for your persecutors.

EIGHTH SUNDAY IN ORDINARY TIME

Isaiah 49: 14-15
1 Corinthians 4: 1-5
Matthew 6: 24-34

Look at the birds in the sky. They do not sow or reap... Learn a lesson from the way the wild flowers grow. They do not work; they do not spin...

Decoration

Make a pretty arrangement in front of the altar today using decorative bird houses and/or bird cages. Add greenery and flowers—maybe putting flowers inside a bird cage and perching ceramic birds on a green branch or at the "entrance" of a bird house. There are many lovely bird houses and cages available today so you should be able to find enough for a very attractive arrangement.

Celebration

Photocopy sheets to be passed out after Mass or placed in the bulletins so they will be taken home. You might use a simple sketch of birds with this headline: *Which is "for the birds"?* Draw a line down the center of the page and to the left put: "Ways I spend my time seeking the riches of the world"; on the right side, put "Ways I spend my time seeking spiritual wisdom and the riches of God's kingdom."

Reflection
We live in a busy, work-oriented world...a world full of schedules, meetings, shopping and trying to catch up and keep up with anyone and everyone who has more than we do. Today's altar decoration reminds us to think of the words of today's Gospel: "Look at the birds in the sky. They do not sow or reap...yet your heavenly Father feeds them. Learn a lesson from the way the wild flowers grow...they do not work or spin yet they are clothed in splendor." How much time do you spend each day, each week, working and worrying about what you will eat or wear, seeking the ways of the world, seeking worldy possessions? How much time do you spend each day, each week, in prayer or Scripture reading or meditation, seeking the ways of holiness, seeking the kingdom of God?

NINTH SUNDAY IN ORDINARY TIME

Deuteronomy 11: 18, 26-28
Romans 3: 21-25, 28
Matthew 7: 21-27

Anyone who hears my words and puts them into practice is like the wise man who built his house on rock. ...Anyone who hears my words but does not put them into practice is like the foolish man who built his house on sandy ground.

Decoration
Cover a low table with a beige cloth and then sprinkle sand on it. Find several pretty ceramic houses (teapots, cream-and- sugars, cookie jars, etc. are often made in this design) and put one of them in the center of the arrangement atop a Bible. Arrange the other houses in the sand and then add branches of greenery on each side to complete the arrangement.

Celebration
If your parish has a Bible study group, ask the leader or a member to come to the pulpit to speak about it briefly and invite parishioners to join—and/or put a notice with information about it in the bulletin. If you do not have such a group, there are many good books available with guidelines for study groups and this would be a good Sunday to invite interested parishioners to "sign up" so you can get one started!

If it is really not possible to start one in your own parish, check with neighboring parishes to see what groups are available and put information about this in the bulletin.

Reflection
You'll notice that the center house in our altar decoration today is sitting atop a Bible—but the other houses are set on sand. This is to remind us of the words of today's gospel when Jesus tells us that anyone who hears his words and puts them into practice is like the wise man who built his house on rock. When the rains and torrents and winds buffeted the house, it did not collapse. But anyone who hears Jesus' words and does *not* put them into practice is like the foolish man who built his house on

sand. When the rains and torrents and winds lashed at it, it *did* collapse. Every Sunday we hear Jesus' words in the Scripture readings but do you remember them or study them to try to understand their meaning so you can put them into practice—so that they can help you when your own house of faith is buffeted by doubts and worldly problems? Some people read the Bible every day and get much spiritual nourishment from it. Others find it very difficult—and even boring—to read the Bible. Maybe the best way to get into the habit of reading Scripture, the best way to learn to understand it and to share it, is to join a Bible study group.

Wouldn't you like to learn more about how to build your house on rock? See the bulletin today for more information.

TENTH SUNDAY IN ORDINARY TIME

Hosea 6: 3-6
Romans 4: 18-25
Matthew 9: 9-13

People who are in good health don't need a doctor; sick people do.

Decoration
Make a long low arrangement of shiny green leaves (magnolia leaves would be attractive or shiny evergreen leaves). In among the leaves, place lots of yellow lemons. Or use a pretty crystal or silver bowl filled with lemons and green leaves. Add yellow candles in crystal or silver candleholders or use yellow votive lights on each side of the arrangement.

Celebration
Have an old-fashioned Lemonade Social today! If weather permits, have it outside on the lawn or parking lot—or have it in the parish hall. Decorate the serving table with another arrangement of leaves and lemons. Serve lemonade from big glass pitchers or punchbowls and have trays of some store-bought lemon-flavored cookies. Ask children to help pass out cups of lemonade and have some happy music playing in the background. If this is not possible, buy lots of wrapped lemon-drop candy and put it in baskets and have children give each person a lemon-drop as they leave Mass.

Reflection
In today's gospel, Jesus has dinner with some tax collectors and sinners! And the Pharisees see this and complain, wondering why the teacher would associate with such undesirables. Jesus says, "People who are in good health do not need a doctor; sick people do." Our altar decoration reminds us that, just like in Jesus' day, there are a lot of "lemons" in our society—a lot of undesirables. It's not just cars that turn out to be lemons—we have to deal with a lot of different kind of "lemons" in everyday life. In fact, most of us would have to admit that we are sometimes the "lemons" ourselves, we are the sick people who need a doc-

tor to help improve our spiritual health. But you know the old saying, "If life hands you a lemon, make lemonade!" So let's remember today that Jesus was willing to associate with lemons like us. To celebrate that fact, we invite you to a Lemonade Social after Mass today in the parish hall (on the front lawn.) We can all think about the lemons in our life as we share a glass of lemonade.

ELEVENTH SUNDAY IN ORDINARY TIME

Exodus 19: 2-6
Romans 5: 6-11
Matthew 9: 36—10:8

*You shall be to me a kingdom of priests, a holy nation. Jesus
sent these men on mission as the Twelve (saying)..go after
the lost sheep of the house of Israel.*

Decoration
Go back to where you packed up that Nativity scene from
Christmas again! If you have some large statues of sheep, use
these in front of the altar with greenery around them. If these are
not available, try to find some kind of ceramic sheep and make
an arrangement of them with greenery on a low table. You might
display them on mirror tiles to make them show up better.

Celebration
Today would be a good day to pray for vocations, for all
priests now working as shepherds to the flock, for once and future priests. Have Benediction and a Holy Hour after the last
Mass or have an afternoon Holy Hour or announce a time to
have a Holy Hour once a month in the future to pray for priests
and vocations. If none of this is possible, put a notice in the bulletin like this: "Today our church is suffering from a lack of shepherds for our flock. We need more vocations to the priesthood
and religious life. Think about that every day this week at your
lunchtime. Pass up that second cup of coffee and use that time
each day to say one or more decades of the rosary to pray for vocations."

Reflection
Today's readings speak to us of the priesthood, the shepherds
of our flock. In the first reading, we hear "You shall be to me a
kingdom of priests, a holy nation." And in the gospel, Jesus is
summoning the Twelve, sending them out to seek the lost sheep.
Our altar decoration reminds us that we, the sheep, need shepherds to lead our flock. Today, our church is suffering from a
lack of vocations. We are told that in only a few years, there may

not be enough priests for every parish to have a pastor. Daily Mass may no longer be possible in all areas. Priests may have to travel from parish to parish to say Sunday Masses. We *must* pray for vocations. We must encourage our own children and other young people to respond if God calls them to the religious life. We must respect the priesthood as a "chosen" way of life. We must pray for the priests who are our shepherds today and ask God to bless us by sending more. As Jesus said in today's gospel, "The harvest is good but laborers are few. Beg the harvest master to send out laborers to gather his harvest."

Twelfth Sunday in Ordinary Time

Jeremiah 20: 10-13
Romans 5: 12-15
Matthew 10: 26-33

*What you hear in private, proclaim from the housetops.
...Whoever acknowledges me before men I will acknowledge
before my Father in heaven.*

Decoration

Do you know any cheerleaders? If so, borrow from them—or
from a school—some of those megaphones that they use to shout
cheers at football games. Use these for your decoration, adding
some flowers and greenery and maybe even some of their colorful cheerleading pom-poms!

Celebration

Announce in the bulletin that next Sunday will be "Welcome"
Sunday for visitors. Challenge parishioners to be cheerleaders
for their church and to proclaim it as Jesus directed. Invite them
to invite others—friends, relatives, neighbors—who are not
Catholics or who may not have been to church for a while to
come to Mass with them next Sunday. Then plan to have a little
"Welcome" breakfast of some kind—donuts and coffee or whatever is convenient. Appoint some "greeters" who will make the
visitors feel welcome and have some Catholic literature on display—pamphlets or magazines or newspapers—available for
visitors to take home free. Maybe you could even prepare some
little "packets" of information and give these to each visitor. In
addition, you could also invite a Sunday School class or some
church group from a neighboring Protestant church to join you
for Welcome Sunday.

Reflection

Our altar decoration today invites us all to be cheerleaders!
Cheerleaders for our church. In the gospel, Jesus tells his apostles, "What you hear in private, *proclaim* from the housetops."
And he also says, "Whoever acknowledges me before men I will
acknowledge before my Father." We Catholics are often hesitant

to *proclaim* our faith, to talk about Jesus to others. When anything else is important in your life, you usually talk about it a lot and share it with your friends—and we should do the same with our religion. Next week, we will have a "Welcome" Sunday and we invite you to invite someone to come to Mass with you—someone who has not been to church in a long time or someone who is not a Catholic. We will have a little "Welcome" coffee after Mass and someone will be on hand to answer any of their questions about our religion. This week, think of someone you could invite, someone you could share the day with—as a way of acknowledging and proclaiming Jesus.

Thirteenth Sunday in Ordinary Time

2 Kings 4: 8-11, 14-16
Romans 6: 3-4, 8-11
Matthew 10: 37-42

He who welcomes you welcomes me, and he who welcomes me welcomes him who sent me.

Decoration
Make a pretty sign in bright colors that simply says, "Welcome." Put it below and in front of the altar and bank flowers and greenery around it.

Celebration
Today you will have the Welcome gathering mentioned last Sunday. Remember to have greeters, someone who can answer questions, free Catholic literature available, and some sort of refreshment like coffee and sweet rolls. You might have some soft background music playing to give it a pleasant atmosphere.

Reflection
In today's gospel, Jesus says, "He who welcomes you welcomes me, and he who welcomes me welcomes him who sent me." Our altar decoration reflects the fact that we would like to extend a special welcome today to our visitors. In the gospel, Jesus also mentions giving a cup of cold water. We would like to invite you to join us after Mass for a cup of water *or* a cup of coffee and a little Welcome breakfast in our parish hall.

FOURTEENTH SUNDAY IN ORDINARY TIME

Zechariah 9: 9-10
Romans 8: 9, 11-13
Matthew 11: 25-30

*Come to me, all you who are weary and find life burden-
some.*

Decoration
Make an arrangement using "care-giver" items—a small tray
holding a glass of water, several pill bottles and a thermometer;
a folded blanket, a hot water bottle, maybe a baby blanket and
baby bottle and a large, windup alarm clock. Intersperse with
greenery.

Celebration
You may not realize how many people in your parish are
weary because of burdensome lives—some are round-the-clock
care-givers, taking care of elderly, handicapped or terminally ill
family members or just trying to adjust to the no-sleep routine of
a baby with colic. These people desperately need just a little time

"away"—to rest and renew their energy. There are probably other parishioners who have time on their hands and may be looking for something to do, a way to feel useful. Today would be a good day to start a *good neighbor network*. Find a chairperson and then put something like this in the bulletin: *"Wanted: Good Neighbors!* Did you know there are some people in our parish who occasionally need just a little neighborly help? Some care for elderly parents, sick relatives, or handicapped children 24-hours a day. They need someone to give-them-a-break just for a couple of hours or for an afternoon or evening—so they can do simple things like shop, get a haircut, go to the dentist or just be free for a little while to rest or sleep. Some young mothers may have no one to help care for a baby or small children when they get sick themselves. If you could give even an hour to help someone like this—or if you *need* help like this—join our Good Neighbor Network. Call _____."

Reflection

In today's gospel, Jesus says "Come to me, all you who are weary and find life burdensome, and I will refresh you." In our busy world, most of us have times when we feel weary or burdened—and often just a few minutes spent in quiet prayer or meditation can bring us spiritual refreshment. But today's altar decoration reminds us that there are also some people in our parish who are burdened by being 24-hour-a-day "care-givers"—people who are caring for sick or elderly or handicapped family members, people who seldom get enough rest and never get any free time to just relax. If you could give "refreshment" by helping—or if you *need* help—please see the bulletin today for information about joining our Good Neighbor Network! And this week, let us all take just a few minutes each day to give our weary, burdensome problems to Jesus in prayer and ask for the "refreshment" of his love and peace.

FIFTEENTH SUNDAY IN ORDINARY TIME

Isaiah 55: 10-11
Romans 8: 18-23
Matthew 13: 1-23 or 13: 1-9

One day a farmer went out sowing...

Decoration
On a low table, covered with a brown cloth, make an arrangement of attractive clear-glass containers. Choose jars, canisters, etc. of varying sizes. Fill each with a different grain—rice, barley, popcorn, etc. Add some small clay pots of herbs—chives, parsley, etc. You might want to turn one or two empty clay pots upside down and set some of the herbs on top of them to give some varied heights to the plants. Or you could just use clippings of ivy arranged around the glass containers.

Celebration
Have a Good-Soil Sale today! Go to a nursery and buy small pots of herbs that can be sold fairly inexpensively. Invite each family to take one home and cultivate it as a family reminder

that we must continue to pray and study in order for our faith to grow and yield a "hundred-fold."

Reflection

Our altar decoration today reminds us of the gospel parable in which Jesus tells of the sowing of the seed—and how some landed on a footpath or on rocky ground or among thorns but that which fell on good soil yielded grain a hundred-fold. Even though the seed of faith has been sown among us, we must guard against the thorns that can choke it out, the passersby that can trample it, the heat of daily troubles that can make it wither away. Today in the vestibule we are having a Good-Soil Sale. We invite you to each take home a small pot of herbs as a reminder that we must continue to pray and study, read Scripture and religious books, in order to nourish and cultivate our faith—so that it too can yield a hundredfold.

SIXTEENTH SUNDAY IN ORDINARY TIME

Wisdom 12: 13, 16-19
Romans 8: 26-27
Matthew 13: 24-43 or 13: 24-30

First collect the weeds and bundle them up to burn, then gather the wheat into my barn.

Decoration

Make an attractive, tall arrangement of flowers or plants and then, in front of it, lay a bunch of dead, dried weeds tied in a bundle. If you are putting this on a low table in front of the altar, use a tablecloth in some color that will contrast to make the dead weeds show up.

Addition—one banner with the design of a glowing, golden sheaf of wheat, a second banner showing a dried, brown, drooping bundle of weeds.

Celebration

Have slips of paper and pencils in the pews and a fireproof container of some kind on the altar (possibly whatever you used on Holy Saturday for the fire.) Ask parishioners to think of the "weeds," the bad habits, the sins that have become a part of their life—the obstacles that could stand between them and salvation. Invite those who choose to do so to write these down on a slip of paper and when they come up to receive the eucharist to drop the slip of paper into the container. At the end of Mass, have the celebrant take the bunch of dried weeds from the altar decoration and put it in the container with the slips of paper and set fire to it so that it will burn as you sing your concluding song.

Reflection

In today's gospel, Jesus tells of the man who sowed good seed but then his enemy came and sowed weeds in the midst of it so that as the crop grew, the weeds grew too. Has an enemy sowed weeds in *your* life? Stop for a minute to think about that today. What weaknesses do you need to weed out—immorality, gluttony, laziness, gossip, disobedience, an indifference to spiritual growth? There are some slips of paper and pencils in the pews

---

and if you would like to, write down one of the things you need to weed out of your life. Then when you come up to receive the eucharist, place the slip of paper in the container by the altar. At the end of Mass, we will take the bundle of weeds in our altar decoration and add it to your weeds and burn them all together to symbolize our desire to weed out the bad in our lives so that the good can grow in us—so that we can be among those gathered into the Father's barn at harvest time.

SEVENTEENTH SUNDAY IN ORDINARY TIME

1 Kings 3: 5, 7-12
Romans 8: 28-30
Matthew 13: 44-52 or 13: 44-46

When he found one really valuable pearl, he went back and
put up for sale all that he had and bought it.

Decoration
Center your decoration with a jewelry case or some decorative container that would look like a "treasure chest." Gather up a lot of pearl costume jewelry and let some long strands of pearls hang out of the side of the chest and drape some in front of it. You could also add other kinds of costume jewelry—gold chains, jeweled pins, etc. Put candles on each side in ornate gold or brass candleholders.

Celebration
Put an announcement similar to this in your bulletin today: "Today's gospel speaks of a treasure chest and a valuable pearl. Do you know someone whose life needs 'enriching,' someone who would 'treasure' a little TLC? Maybe a lonely friend or relative desperately needs some of your time and attention right now. Maybe someone in the parish who hasn't been able to get to church lately would be enriched if you brought them one of today's announcement sheets plus a pamphlet or booklet to read—and maybe a coffeecake or a few cookies! Think of some way you could be a 'treasure' to someone this week."

Reflection
Today's readings speak to us of understanding. In the first reading, God tells Solomon to ask for anything he wants and God will give it to him. Solomon asks only for an "understanding heart"—so that he may know right from wrong. In the second reading, we hear that "God makes all things work together for the good of those who love him." And of course, the gospel tells the familiar story of one man finding buried treasure and another man finding a valuable pearl. Each of them sells all he has in order to purchase the treasure. What *is* the only treasure

worth owning? God's love and wisdom, God's kingdom. But are we willing to give up all we have in order to own this treasure? Are we willing to see the foolish things of earth as only temporary pleasures and keep always in mind the eternal truth, the eternal treasure? This week, meditate on the words of the gospel, "The reign of God is like a buried treasure which a man found in a field....rejoicing, he sold all that he had and bought that field."

EIGHTEENTH SUNDAY IN ORDINARY TIME

Isaiah 55: 1-3
Romans 8: 35, 37-39
Matthew 14: 13-21

All you who have no money, come, receive grain and eat. All those present ate their fill.

Decoration
Use a brass or glass container and fill it with a "bouquet" of fresh vegetables—red tomatoes, yellow squash, purple eggplant, etc. For "greenery," use leaf lettuce, parsley or mint.

Addition—banners with the design of loaves and fishes.

Celebration
Since today's readings speak of feeding the multitudes, this would be a good time to ask for food donations for the poor. Put a "Food" basket in the vestibule of the church where people can leave canned goods or non-perishables all through the year for distribution by the St. Vincent de Paul Society or some other parish group.

Reflection

Today's readings speak of nourishment, of feeding the multitudes. The first reading says, "Come to the water...come, receive grain and eat" and the gospel story is that of the crowds Jesus fed by sharing the five loaves and two fish. Our altar decoration reflects the bounty of our gardens, the rich harvest of our fields. But as we give thanks for our own blessings, we should remember those who are less fortunate, those who seldom have the opportunity to "eat their fill." We have placed a "Food" basket in the vestibule and ask you to remember the less fortunate by filling it with any kind of canned goods or non-perishable food items which you could share. The St. Vincent de Paul Society will take whatever food is donated each week and distribute it to needy families. In this way, our parish can show our concern and compassion, as Jesus did, by sharing in a small way the apostolate of feeding the multitudes.

NINETEENTH SUNDAY IN ORDINARY TIME

1 Kings 19: 9, 11-13
Romans 9: 1-5
Matthew 14: 22-23

Peter got out of the boat and began to walk on the water moving toward Jesus...but...becoming frightened, he began to sink and cried out "Lord, save me!" Jesus at once stretched out his hand and caught him.

Decoration

Instead of a cloth today, cover the top of a small table with mirror tiles to simulate water. Add greenery at the edges and simply center a boat in the middle.

Addition—a blue banner with the design of stormy waves in white, a white banner with the outline design of a boat in blue.

Celebration

Does your parish have a Lending Library of books plus audio and video tapes? If you do, today would be the day to encourage parishioners to check out some faith-builders. If you don't, this would be a good time to start one by asking for donations of spiritual books and tapes. All you need is a few book shelves in a quiet corner of a hall where you can display the books, plus a card file or just a notebook so that people can write down their name when they take out or return a book. You might want to keep the videotapes and audio tapes at the rectory since you will need to keep closer track of them—but be sure they are easily accessible to parishioners.

Reflection

In today's gospel, we see Peter actually walking across water toward Jesus! Then when he realizes how stormy the waters are, he becomes panicky and cries for help. Jesus saves him but says, "How little faith you have. Why did you falter?" What would you do if Jesus asked you to walk on water? Would you be any braver or have more faith than Peter? We all start out bravely but as soon as things get stormy, most of us falter. And the only way we can bolster this weak, easily-threatened faith is to continue to work on it and try to strengthen it. To help you become more faith-filled, our parish has (is beginning) a parish Lending Library of books, videotapes, and audiotapes. See the bulletin for more information about how to donate or how to check out faith-boosters! And let us all pray that we will be able to grow in our spiritual commitment so Jesus will not have to look at us and say, "How little faith you have. Why did you falter?"

Twentieth Sunday in Ordinary Time

Isaiah 56: 1, 6-7
Romans 11: 13-15, 29-32
Matthew 15: 21-28

Lord, Son of David, have pity on me! My daughter is terribly troubled by a demon.

Decoration

Use the theme of rainbows today! Cut colored strips of crepe paper to make the rainbow effect or use any of the many rainbow decorations available in the stores today. Possibly center the arrangement with a small sign lettered, "Rainbows for All God's Children."

Addition—a banner made with the cloud, rainbow and sunshine "logo" of this program.

Celebration

"Rainbows for All God's Children" is a national support group program to help children who are grieving because they have suffered an important loss in their life—by death, divorce, moving to a new area away from family and friends, etc. It is not a counseling or therapy session but strictly a peer support group—for either grade school or high school children—led by volunteer parishioners who will be trained to guide them. Since today's gospel tells of the woman whose daugher was "troubled by a demon," this would be a good Sunday to introduce this program to your parish. For information about how to organize this program, write to: Rainbows for All God's Children, 1111 Tower Road, Schaumburg, IL 60173. Or call 312-310-1880.

Reflection

Today's gospel tells of the woman whose daughter was "terribly troubled by a demon." She kept begging Jesus for help until his disciples were irritated and wanted to get rid of her. But Jesus said to her, "You have great faith! Your wish will come to pass." And at that moment, her daughter got better. Our altar decoration of rainbows announces that we will begin a program in our parish that is designed to help children who are "terribly troubled" and grieving. The program, called "Rainbows for All God's Children," helps children who are grieving because they have suffered a serious loss in their life—through death, divorce, or other "troubling demons" in our society. If you would like to help with this program, please see the bulletin for more information.

TWENTY-FIRST SUNDAY IN ORDINARY TIME

Jeremiah 38: 4-6, 8-10
Hebrews 12: 1-4
Luke 12: 49-53

Who do you say that I am?

Decoration
Use a pretty quilt today as a "table cloth"—to indicate the beautiful and endless variety of ways in which Jesus touches the lives of his people. Depending on your altar, you might want to use a smaller size quilt—like those made for baby beds. You

could add an arrangement of greenery in the middle but nothing too busy to detract from the quilt pattern. Or you might choose to use several quilt "blocks" in different patterns. Or simply drape a quilt over a stool in front of the altar or over an antique rocking chair to the side of the altar. Quilting is so popular to-day, you should be able to find a variety of ways to incorporate this idea into your decoration—using whatever quilted items are available.

Addition—hang some attractive quilted "wall-hangings" as banners.

Celebration
Ask a class in the parish school or PSR program or some parish organization to make bookmarks for today, enough to give one to each parishioner. Each bookmark should have the message, "Who do you say that I am?"

Just use colored construction paper, posterboard, felt or whatever's available. To make the project simpler, you could make a "master," drawing the bookmark design and then just run these off on colored paper. Then all your "volunteers" would have to do is cut out the bookmarks! You could draw a "quilt" pattern for the top border.

Reflection
Today's quilt decoration illustrates the infinite variety of God—and of his people. In today's gospel, Jesus asks, "Who do people say the Son of Man is?" And he is told that they all have different answers—some say John the Baptist, others Elijah or Jeremiah or one of the prophets. Then Jesus asks, "Who do *you* say that I am?" The lives of God's people are each unique—there are different patterns and textures and colors and designs—and all joined together, like in a patchwork quilt, they make something beautiful. But because of this variety, this difference, each of us may have a different answer to the question, "Who do you say that I am?" Think about that question this week. Think how you would answer if Jesus stood before you and asked it.

TWENTY-SECOND SUNDAY IN ORDINARY TIME

Jeremiah 20: 7-9
Romans 12: 1-2
Matthew 16: 21-27

What profit would a man show if he were to gain the whole world and ruin himself in the process?

Decoration
Today, use the theme of the light and fire of God's word which every person is commissioned to spread. To make "candles" to hang behind the altar, buy some of those inexpensive, colorful, fringed mats or rugs (that you might use as a throw-rug in your front hall or inside the kitchen door). Put two together to make tall "candles" and use only one for a shorter candle. Add "candle flames" of stiff yellow and orange paper. (If you can't find the rugs, you could simply use a globe as the focus of your decoration today, adding greenery and a grouping of candles or vigil lights on each side.)

Celebration

Perhaps you could have small candles in the pews today and at the Intercession time, ask all to light these candles. Then ask each person to think of what worldly thing in his or her life could get in the way of spreading the light and fire of God's words. Ask each to pray in silence to find a way to extinguish this and start this day to be filled with the fire and light of God's love and to try to pass it on to others. Or pass out these small candles at the door for everyone to take home as a reminder.

Reflection

In today's first reading, Jeremiah says that the word of the Lord "becomes like fire burning in my heart." And in the gospel, Jesus reminds us, "Whoever would save his life would lose it but whoever loses his life for my sake will find it." Our altar decoration reminds us that our hearts must be on fire with the word of the Lord, ready to carry the light of his message to the world, no matter how difficult or "inconvenient" it might be in today's materialistic world that constantly lures us away from God's teachings. This week, think about what there is in your world that *keeps* you from spreading the light, the fire, the message of Christianity. Consider how you might change that as you recall Jesus' other words in the gospel, "What profit would a man show if he were to gain the whole world and ruin himself in the process?"

Twenty-Third Sunday in Ordinary Time

Ezekiel 33: 7-9
Romans 13: 8-10
Matthew 18: 15-20

If you do not speak out to dissuade the wicked man from his ways, he shall die from his guilt but I will hold you responsible. If your brother should commit some wrong against you, go and point out his fault, but keep it between the two of you.

Decoration
Use either a black and white striped cloth today to simulate prison bars or a plain black cloth. Center it with an arrangement of lengths of heavy chains and locks. If you can find a piece of grillwork made of bars, you could include that.

Celebration
Have you heard of the prison ministry called "Loving Contact?" A young Catholic mother of nine, who suffers from multiple sclerosis, decided to use the "quiet time" demanded by her illness to write letters to prisoners. This grew into a newsletter and finally into a booklet of about 40 pages which she sends out *free* every month to prisoners all across the country. Titled "Loving Contact," it includes art work, poems, pen-pal requests and articles written BY prisoners plus puzzles, quizes, and inspirational notes *for* prisoners. In recognition of her work, she received the Woman's Day Magazine "Outstanding Woman Award" but her favorite "awards" are prisoners' letters of gratitude and renewed faith. You could put a notice in the bulletin today about this ministry with the address where parishioners can send requests for someone to be placed on the mailing list to receive this FREE booklet (or to send donations since money is always short.) The address is: Loving Contact Prison Ministries, P. O. Box 226, Herscher, IL 60941

Reflection
Today's readings speak of evil ways, of law and injustice. In the first reading, Ezekiel says we are "watchmen" who should speak out to try to dissuade the wicked man from his ways. The

second reading tells us that "he who loves his neighbor has fulfilled the law." And in the gospel, Jesus tells his disciples what to do if someone commits a wrong against them. In keeping with this, our altar decoration reminds us of our "brothers" who have committed wrong and must now spend time behind bars. All too often we easily dismiss such people and forget to include them in our prayers or good works. One young Catholic mother did not forget them. She has started a prison ministry to remind prisoners that "God does not care what you have *been*, only what you can *become* in his love." Her ministry is called "Loving Contact" and it has helped hundreds of prisoners find God again. If you would like to help her spread this ministry, see the notice in today's bulletin. And this week, say a prayer for prisoners as you recall Jesus' parting words in today's gospel, "If two of you join your voices on earth to pray for anything whatever, it shall be granted you by my Father in heaven."

Twenty-Fourth Sunday in Ordinary Time

Sirach 27: 30-28
Romans 14: 7-9
Matthew 18: 21-35

How often must I forgive...seven times? ...seventy times seven times."

Decoration

Make an arrangement of some "unusual" flowers—thistles, flowering mint, wild flowers or simple sun flowers. Place this next to a chest or box on which you have attached a sign lettered "St. Monica League." And, if you can find one, add a picture of St. Monica with her son, St. Augustine.

Addition—banner with the design of praying hands.

Celebration

St. Monica is known for her long years of praying for her husband and son to return to God. Since many Catholics today have children or relatives who have left the Church, why not start a St. Monica League to pray for their return. You don't have to have meetings or luncheons or do anything but ask people to promise to pray. Invite parishioners to write down names of those who are no longer "active" for whom they would like to request prayers and drop them in the St. Monica League box. Include the St. Monica League "members" in your petitions each Sunday and possibly have a monthly Holy Hour when you place the chest or box on the altar and pray together for everyone whose name has been included.

Reflection

In today's first reading, we are reminded, "wrath and anger are hateful things...forgive your neighbor's injustice." And the gospel reminds us to forgive seventy times seven times. In every life, there are many chances to forgive—and sometimes in families, it truly seems it must be seventy times seven. Today's altar decoration reminds us of St. Monica, a mother who forgave and prayed for years for the conversion of her husband and son. Her prayers were finally answered and her son became St. Augustine. Today, many Catholics have children or relatives who no longer practice their faith and maybe even criticize and ridicule the church they once loved. As a faith community, we should forgive them and pray they will forgive us. One way to do this is by forming a St. Monica League. Simply write down the name of anyone for whom you wish prayers and drop their name in the box on the altar. Each week we will join to pray for them as St. Monica prayed for her family.

TWENTY-FIFTH SUNDAY IN ORDINARY TIME

Isaiah 55: 6-9
Philippians 1: 20-24, 27
Matthew 20: 1-16

The owner of an estate went out at dawn to hire workmen for his vineyard...he came out about midmorning and saw other men...he came out again at noon and midafternoon and did the same ...finally, in late afternoon he found still others ...

Decoration

For your decoration, use several clocks set at different times— 6, 9, 12, 2, 5. Arrange them at different heights and surround them with ivy or other greenery.

Addition—banners with the design of clock faces, shaded in to indicate various hours.

Celebration

Get those volunteers busy again! Make large round cardboard clock faces with hands pointing to various times and hang these on the walls down the side aisles and/or on all the church doors so people cannot fail to notice them as they are coming through the doors.

Reflection

Our altar decoration reflects today's familiar gospel reading in which we hear the story of the man who hired workers for his vineyard. Each came to work at a different time yet each received the same pay. The workers who worked the longest grumbled and questioned the man and he replied, "Are you envious because I am generous?" Like the vineyard owner, God is most generous to all of us—yet sometimes it seems that he is *more* generous with others than he is with us and so we begin to grumble and complain. But we cannot see into the hearts of men and we cannot understand the ways of God. This week, let us replace jealousy with gratitude for God's great generosity. Instead of grumbling or waiting for the "right time," let us turn to him at *all* hours of the day and night, recalling the words of today's first reading—"Seek the Lord while he may be found, call him while he is near."

Twenty-Sixth Sunday in Ordinary Time

Ezekiel 18: 25-28
Philippians 2: 1-11 or 2: 1-5
Matthew 21: 28-32

Which of the two did what the father wanted?

Decoration

"Layer" your table today! Use different-sized and different-patterned tablecloths and layer them. Have a flowered or lace one on the bottom and then cover it with other cloths draped diagonally—using stripes, checks, patterns, etc. You can center this with a simple arrangement of greenery or a flower arrangement using only one color flower so that you will not detract from the cloths.

Celebration

Go to a fabric store and buy bags of "scraps" of material that are usually used by quilters. Have children hold baskets of these and pass them out to all parishioners after each Mass as a reminder of the "cover-up," the pretense, of righteousness.

Reflection

Today's gospel presents another parable, another puzzle. Jesus tells of the man who asked his two sons to go and work in his vineyard. One responded "yes" immediately—but then did not go. The other said "no" but later repented and *did* go. Our many-layered altar decoration reminds us of how often we "cover-up" our true intentions. Many people profess loudly to be Christians but do not live a Christian life. Others may seem to reject Christ's teachings but eventually repent and do great work in his vineyard. As you leave today, you will each receive a little scrap of fabric, a reminder to ask yourself if your life is a "cover-up," a pretense. Is your religion on the outside only? Are you fooling others *and* yourself? Or do you have a genuine commitment to live a Christian life and go forth to work in the master's vineyard?

Twenty-Seventh Sunday in Ordinary Time

Isaiah 5: 1-7
Philippians 4: 6-9
Matthew 21: 33-43

When vintage time arrived, he dispatched his slaves to the tenants to obtain his share of the grapes.

Decoration
Use a nice lace or solid-color cloth today and center it with a large, attractive basket filled to the brim with lots of greenery and lots of bunches of either real or artificial grapes in various colors.

Celebration
In the vestibule, have a table with baskets of real grapes—possibly several different varieties—cut into small clusters of just 3 or 4 grapes each. Invite parishioners to "help themselves" to a few grapes as a reminder of today's story of the vineyard.

Reflection
In today's gospel reading, God owns a vineyard but the tenants of it refuse to acknowledge his ownership. Even when he sends his own son, they kill him and reject him. Do we sometimes act this way too? Do we refuse to acknowledge that the world belongs to God and we are only tenants? Do we reject Jesus, the son of God, by refusing to follow the guidelines for living which he gave to us? Stop by the vestibule today to sample a small bunch of grapes as a reminder that we are not the owners of the vineyard but only the tenants, the stewards who should protect and cultivate it so that it will yield a rich harvest.

Twenty-Eighth Sunday in Ordinary Time

Isaiah 25: 6-10
Philippians 4: 12-14, 19-20
Matthew 22: 1-14 or 22: 1-10

He dispatched his servants to summon the invited guests to the wedding but they refused to come.

Decoration
Cover a small table with a white cloth and center it with a pretty arrangement of white flowers. Then add "poufs" of white net and stand up engraved wedding invitations amidst the net. (If you know a family who has had a recent wedding, they may have leftover invitations to give you or you could go to a print shop and ask if they have any samples they could give you.)

Celebration
Have you ever gone to a wedding where they gave the guests little "packages" of rice to toss? Perhaps you could make enough of these to pass out after Mass—as a reminder of the wedding feast in the gospel. Just take a small square of nylon net and put a spoonful of rice on it. Then gather up the net and tie a ribbon round it to make a tiny little round ball of rice. Put all the pretty little packets into a basket and distribute!

Reflection
In today's gospel, the reign of God is compared to a wedding feast. Our altar decoration reminds us that we are all invited—but will some of us refuse to come like the guests in the parable? Will we be too busy, too disinterested? Might we even ridicule the servants of the master—the teachers, the priests— who try to encourage us to come? Today as you leave, you will receive a little packet of wedding rice. Keep it in your pocket this week as a reminder that you have been invited to a wonderful wedding feast. How will you reply to the invitation? Will you accept or reject your invitation?

Twenty-Ninth Sunday in Ordinary Time

Isaiah 45: 1, 4-6
1 Thessalonians 1: 1-5
Matthew 22: 15-21

The Pharisees went off and began to plot how they might trap Jesus in speech.

Decoration
In today's shops, you can find many beautiful stained glass "light catchers." Some stand on their own, some are to be hung. Find some of these and make an attractive arrangement of them and then position a candle behind each one so that the light will shine through and make the colors sparkle and the design show up. Add a bit of greenery at the sides.

Celebration
Perhaps the best celebration today would be just to suggest some quiet thinking-and-listening time!

Reflection
Have you ever looked at stained glass from the outside, from the wrong side? From that perspective, the colors look all muddled, the picture is indistinguishable. But when you step *inside* and see the light shining through the glass, the colors become brilliant and the design of the picture is clear. Today's altar decoration of stained glass reflects the instance in today's gospel when the Pharisees plotted to trap Jesus and he responded by saying, "Why are you trying to trip me up, you hypocrites?" So often today our world tries to trap us and trip us up. We get muddled and it becomes hard to see the picture clearly, to see the brilliant colors of God's love, to see the clear difference between right and wrong. Step aside today and spend a little quiet time to think of that. Let God's light shine through. Listen. Pay attention. Think of the muddled messages the world has been giving you. Ask God to help you see the picture more clearly so that you can avoid the trap and not get tripped up.

THIRTIETH SUNDAY IN ORDINARY TIME

Exodus 2: 20-26
1 Thessalonians 1: 5-10
Matthew 22: 34-40

You shall love your neighbor as yourself.

Decoration
Have you noticed how many interesting boxes and bags are available today? Some gift "containers" are almost as interesting as the gift! Gather together a collection of colorful wood, enamel, straw, metal, paper or whatever boxes or containers. Make an attractive arrangement of them, interspersing it with greenery, flowers or candles.

Addition—one or more banners, using the design of colorfully-wrapped gift boxes, trimmed with bows, ribbon streamers, etc. and possibly some sequins or glitter.

Celebration
The idea of having a "Secret Pal" used to be quite popular—and today seems like a good time to revive it! Put a little notice in your bulletin to this effect: Have you ever had a Secret Pal? In today's gospel, we are told to "love your neighbor as yourself" so this week would be the perfect time to become a Secret Pal! Look around your neighborhood—or your family—and see if you don't find someone who is lonely or sick or tired, someone who could use a little cheering-up. "Adopt" that person! Send greeting cards, surprise them with little gifts—a batch of cookies, a small plant, a bag of home-grown tomatoes or even something fun like bubblegum! Keep it a secret—Or let them know you are thinking of them by stopping by for a visit or inviting them to go somewhere with you and your family. No matter how young or how old you are, you can be a Secret Pal—and you may be surprised to find that *you* get as much joy from it as the person who becomes your pal!

Reflection
Today's decoration of boxes and containers suggests the idea of a secret. We all love secrets—so how about becoming a Secret

Pal! In today's gospel, we are told to love God with your whole heart, soul and mind. But we are also told to love your neighbor as yourself—and sometimes that's even harder! This week, look around at your neighborhood or maybe your own family and see if there isn't someone who could use a little extra Tender Loving Care. Then become that person's *secret* Pal! For more information about how to become a Pal, see today's bulletin. And this week, remember what Jesus answered when he was asked, "Which commandment of the law is the greatest?"

Thirty-First Sunday in Ordinary Time

Malachi 1: 14-2, 2: 8-10
1 Thessalonians 2: 7-9, 13
Matthew 23: 1-12

Their words are bold but their deeds are few.

Decoration
How about a decoration today of radios—those little boxes from which "words" spew forth constantly! There are radios made in all sorts of shapes and sizes so gather together a variety of them and make an arrangement, adding the usual greenery and/or flowers and candles.

Celebration
In today's bulletin, put this suggestion: "Do something daring this week! Turn off the radio! Both in your car and at home! If you feel really daring, turn off the television too! Surround yourself with quiet! In today's gospel, Jesus speaks of the scribes and Pharisees and says, 'Their words are bold but their deeds are few.' When you turn off all those unnecessary, bold radio and television 'words,' you can use that quiet time to pray and listen for God's words. You may be surprised at what you 'hear' in the silence!"

Reflection
When Jesus speaks of the scribes and Pharisees in today's gospel, it sounds like he could be speaking of some of the people in our world today. He says, "Their words are bold but their deeds are few....they put heavy burdens on *other* people but don't lift a finger themselves...they seek the places of honor and the front seats and want everyone to notice how important they are."

Today's altar decoration reminds us of how we are so bombarded with 'bold words' and new ideas and false leadership from the media—when what we need might be a bit of silence and God's peace. And so we challenge you to try something daring this week. See the bulletin for details of this quiet challenge!

Thirty-Second Sunday in Ordinary Time

Wisdom 6: 12-16
1Thessalonians 4: 13-18 or 4: 13-14
Matthew 25: 1-13

The ones who were ready went into the wedding with him.

Decoration
Today make a nice center arrangement of colorful flowers—possibly even a French bouquet or something that might suggest a bridesmaid's bouquet! On one side, put several tall vigil or sanctuary lights that are lit. On the other side, have unlit "empty" lights (use some that have already been used and are burned down).

Addition—one banner with the design of ten torches, another with the design of four or five flasks labeled "oil."

Celebration
Perhaps today you could give each person a small vigil light to take home. Put a note in the bulletin, suggesting that they light the vigil light each day and say a short prayer that they will be "prepared" when the groom comes.

Reflection
Are you "prepared?" Keep your eyes open for you know not the day or the hour. In today's gospel, some of the bridesmaids plan ahead and bring extra flasks of oil to keep their torches lit. Others are not prepared. They are not ready to go in with him when the groom comes. How can we prepare today? Perhaps through prayer, meditation, Scripture reading, saying the rosary, attending daily Mass. Today we invite you each to take a small vigil light home with you. Light it each day this week and meditate on the words of today's gospel. Ask God to help you prepare so that you will be ready when the groom comes.

Thirty-Third Sunday in Ordinary Time

Proverbs 31: 10-13, 19-20, 30-31
1 Thessalonians 5: 1-6
Matthew 25: 14-30 or 25: 14-15, 19-20

A man called in his servants and handed his funds over to them according to each man's abilities.

Decoration

Make a "baptismal" arrangement today! Use white flowers, a baby's white baptismal gown, a baptismal candle, a container of water, etc.

Addition—one banner with the design of coins falling from an old-time money pouch, another with the design of water falling from a shell or dipper.

Celebration

Perhaps at each Mass, you could ask of those present, who was baptized the longest time ago—70 years ago, 80? Give that person a flower or a small bag of gold candy "coins." Then ask who was baptized the most recently—a month ago, a week ago? And give the same gift to that person (it will probably be a baby and you will present the gift to the mother—but who knows, it *could* be an adult!).

Reflection

In today's gospel, the master shares his money with his servants according to each one's ability. Then the master goes away and when he returns, he is pleased to see that some of them have used the share wisely, have invested it and made it grow. In the same way, when we were baptized, God shared his life with us and he expects us to invest it wisely and to make our faith grow. Our altar decoration reminds us of that baptism. Since you received those saving waters which gave you a share of God's life, have you used that life wisely? Have you invested it and worked to make your faith grow?

FEAST OF CHRIST THE KING

Ezekiel 34: 11-12, 15-17
1 Corinthians 15: 20-26, 28
Matthew 25: 31-46

As often as you neglected to do it to one of these least ones,
you neglected to do it to me.

Decoration
Make the central focus of today's decoration a gold crown, possibly studded with "jewels" and placed on a velvet pillow and flanked with greenery and/or candles in golden candelabra. But then make "sign posts"—or banners with the design of sign posts. One post should have signs pointing to "St. Louis, San Francisco, New York, Nashville" or some of the cities in your vicinity. The other should have signs pointing to "Charity, Compassion, Social Justice, Alms," etc.

Celebration
If it is possible to make the posts, have someone carry them in today in procession and place them at each side of the altar to complement the Crown decoration. Even if you use the banners, you could possibly have someone carry them in procession and then hang them.

Reflection
Today we celebrate the Feast of Christ the King. And what *is* a king? A ruler, a protector, a leader who directs and guides the lives of his people. In today's gospel, Jesus gives us all "directions," a signpost that points to the way we should live our lives. And Jesus' directions are not lenghty or complicated. He simply says, "Feed the hungry....give water to those who thirst...clothe the naked...welcome the lonely...give compassion to those who are imprisoned...console the sick and grieving." Are you following the directions of your leader, living by the guidelines given to you by your King?